RHIANNON

# JAGUAR WOMAN

Also by Lynn V. Andrews

MEDICINE WOMAN
FLIGHT OF THE SEVENTH MOON:
The Teaching of the Shields

# JAGUAR
# WOMAN

## And the Wisdom of
## the Butterfly Tree

*Lynn V. Andrews*

1817

Harper & Row, Publishers, San Francisco

Cambridge, Hagerstown, New York, Philadelphia,
London, Mexico City, São Paulo, Singapore, Sydney

Acknowledgement is made for permission to reprint the following: "Jaguar Woman" by Jack Crimmins, copyright © 1985 by Jack Crimmins; used with permission of the author. "I Always Return to this Place" from *The Collected Works of Kenneth Patchen*, by Kenneth Patchen, copyright © 1945 by Kenneth Patchen; reprinted by permission of New Directions Publishing Corp. "The Jewel" from *Collected Poems*, by James Wright, copyright © 1962 by Wesleyan University Press; reprinted by permission of Wesleyan University Press. "Theology" from *Ring of Bone*, by Lew Welch, copyright © 1979 by Grey Wolf Press; reprinted by permission of Grey Wolf Press. "The Final Mother" by Jack Crimmins, copyright © 1985 by Jack Crimmins; used with permission of the author. "For Shirley and Wallace" from *Jaguar Skies*, by Michael McClure, copyright © 1975 by Michael McClure; reprinted by permission of New Directions Publishing Corp. "Oh No" from *For Love, Poems 1950–1960*, by Robert Creeley, copyright © 1962 by Robert Creeley; reprinted by permission of Charles Scribner's Sons. "The Presence" from *The Jacob's Ladder*, by Denise Levertov, copyright © 1961 by Denise Levertov Goodman; reprinted by permission of New Directions Publishing Corp. "Circling" from *Living in the Open*, by Marge Piercy, copyright © 1976 by Marge Piercy; reprinted by permission of Alfred A. Knopf Inc. "Suppose" from *Desire Being Full of Distances*, by Elizabeth Herron, copyright © 1983 by Elizabeth Herron; reprinted by permission of the author. "Route" from *Collected Poems*, by George Oppen, copyright © 1968 by George Oppen; reprinted by permission of New Directions Publishing Corp. From *The Benevolent Song of Earthbound Beings*, by Philip Daughtry, copyright © 1985 by Philip Daughtry; reprinted by permission of the author. "Come into Animal Presence" from *The Jacob's Ladder*, by Denise Levertov, copyright © 1961 by Denise Levertov Goodman; reprinted by permission of New Directions Publishing Corp. "Grandmother" from *Coyote's Daylight Trip*, by Paula Gunn Allen, copyright © 1978 by Paula Gunn Allen; reprinted by permission of the author. From "The Tree in the Dark" by Sheila Ross, copyright © 1985 by Sheila Ross; used with permission of the author.

Designed by Don Hatch

Library of Congress Cataloging in Publication Data
Andrews, Lynn V.
    Jaguar woman and the wisdom of the butterfly tree.
    1. Andrews, Lynn V. 2. Whistling Elk, Agnes.
3. Creek Indians—Religion and mythology.    4. Indians
of North America—Great Plains—Religion and
mythology.    5. Indians of Mexico—Religion and
mythology.    6. Women and religion. I. Title.
E99.C88A527    1985    299'.78    84–48762
ISBN 0–06–250029–5

85  86  87  88  89  MPC  10  9  8  7  6  5  4  3  2

*To the memory of Opal Carson
and for the native peoples of the Yucatan and Central America.*

*Special thanks to Martine Prechtel and his wife, Dolores.*

This is a true story.
Some of the names and places in this book
have been changed to protect the privacy of those involved.

# Table of Contents

. . . if a woman does a useless thing, none reproves her; if she does a
harmful thing, few seek to restrain her; but if she seeks to imitate the
goddess and to encourage others, all those in authority accuse her of
corruption. So it is more dangerous to teach truth than to enter a powder
magazine with a lighted torch.

Tsiang Samdup
The Book of Sayings

Jaguar Woman speaking
like fire.

With an eye of smoke
and a daggered hand: she.

Like stars
black sky obsidian
    *loops of light*
    *moon light star light*
    *all night long*

She is the marrow of the underbrush.
She is the waterfall no one has seen.
She is the resting place of the sun.

Extend the universe in every direction
and bring her home.

Jack Crimmins
"Jaguar Woman"

# Preface

Since 1973 I have been traveling to Manitoba, Canada, to see a certain Native American medicine woman named Agnes Whistling Elk. At first I came to her as an art dealer from Los Angeles in search of a sacred marriage basket. Slowly our relationship changed, and I became this woman's apprentice. She has taught me a system of beliefs that had previously been foreign to me.

Agnes stresses the dignity and value of womanhood. She has said that it had been told to her in prophecy that I was to become a warrioress of the rainbow of black, white, red, and yellow peoples, and that one day I would become a bridge between the two distinct worlds of the primal mind and the white consciousness.

During the course of my apprenticeship, I have been forced to restructure my beliefs as to who I am and what the world is. In an alien environment I was pitted against an adept male sorcerer named Red Dog. In this dangerous struggle I triumphed, much to my surprise. I have undergone several initiations since then, culminating with an initiation into a highly secretive shamanistic society of women known as the Sisterhood of the Shields.

Agnes asked me to write about these experiences, to "let the eagle fly," and to teach people in an effort to heal our sacred Mother Earth. *Medicine Woman* was my first attempt to do this, and *Flight of the Seventh Moon* was the second in a series of books about the extraordinary adventures and shamanistic teachings I have encountered. These books stress the ancient powers of woman. This ancient knowledge has been memorized and beaded into history by powerful Native women throughout time in order to protect and preserve it for the generations that follow on this beautiful earth.

*Jaguar Woman* explores a range of movement, much as the

butterfly covers this continent in its wanderings from Canada to
Mexico. This book explores not only a physical change of locale, but
also the process of psychic, mental, and emotional movement from
one state of mind to another, and movement from one attribute of
perception to another.

One of the great tools of the Native American tradition is the
medicine wheel. This seemingly simple existential paradigm is a rich,
complex, and subtle symbol of mystical and philosophical depth.
Trained apprentices are taught to use the medicine wheel as a map
to their innermost being. The four directions on the wheel represent
categories of qualities both inner and outer: the south represents
trust and innocence; the west is the home of the sacred dream,
death, and rebirth; the north symbolizes wisdom and strength; and
the east is illumination.

The key to using the medicine wheel is movement, the way a
person moves from one direction to another in the process of
learning. For example, a woman living in trust and innocence in the
south of the medicine wheel may progress through a series of life
experiences and reach a state of wisdom and strength in the north.
At this point of wisdom she has grown from a life of materialism
represented in the south to a position of spirit represented in the
north. The key to evolving further is, again, movement. Because she
has gone from the south looking north for the spirit, she must now
move from the north looking south to manifest substance. After
manifesting substance, she must then travel back north to manifest
spirit, and so on.

This book describes my lessons of transit, and my meeting with
the Sisterhood of the Shields in pursuit of knowledge and the
adventure of the spirit. I again traveled north to meet my teachers,
Agnes Whistling Elk and Ruby Plenty Chiefs in northern Manitoba,
Canada. My experiences took me to the center of the sacred spiral
in order to reclaim my original female nature—the real woman
within.

"There are no excuses for anything," Agnes once told me. "You
change things or you don't. Excuses rob you of power and induce
apathy."

I sometimes see women who have been cheated out of their spiritual heritage just as they have been cheated out of their minds and bodies. I, for one, struggle against that theft.

L.V.A.
Red Deer
Alberta, Canada
August 1984

I always return to the Mystery . . .
And I think there is nothing in the world but the Mystery.

Kenneth Patchen
"I Always Return to This Place"

# Chapter 1
# Dream Journey to the North

The aurora borealis streaked across the cloudless sky. Great flashes of green and purple pulsated in swordlike patterns—a noiseless celebration of moving color above the stark, frozen tundra that stretched endlessly before us. The runners of the dogsled sliced through the virgin snow, making an odd whirring sound. The ten huskies pulling our sled had lapsed into silent running. The dogs had barked and yowled joyously earlier in the day, but now they were tired. Although I had been over this trail many times earlier in the year, if Ruby Plenty Chiefs' apprentice, July, a young Cree woman, had not been with me now I would have been completely lost.

The wind cut out of the north, leaving my face frozen and numb, and snow crystals brushed against my cheeks. I turned away from the persistent gale. The snow had formed a hard white rim on the fur edging my parka hood. Even in the afternoon glow, the sleeping trees sticking out at angles from the snowdrifts looked gray and bleak, barely throwing shadows. Occasionally, a larger tree trunk would reflect the red in the sky, pulsating for a moment with an eerie dance of hidden life borrowed from another season, and then quickly flash back into gray anonymity.

July and I had each been pushing behind the sled with one foot and riding on a runner with the other. For July this was a way of life. For me it was a tremendous effort. As we hurtled forward over

the snow, the sled began to jerk and drag. Sensing the exhaustion of
the dogs, July called the team to a halt.

We squatted down beneath a rise of snow, huddling together for
warmth. July got out a can of sterno and lit it with a lighter. We
waved our mittened hands over the flame. Then July took her
sheath knife and sliced off a bite from a frozen fish. She handed a
large morsel to me. I gnawed on the first nourishment I had had in
hours, ignoring the odd taste and texture, thankful for the food and
rest. July squinted at the sky, assessing our position. Ominous storm
clouds were gathering in the distance.

July turned to me, grinning impishly. Her twenty-three-year-old
brown face was beautiful. She said, "You picked a fine time to travel
north." She gestured toward the black cathedral of clouds moving in
our direction. "Why didn't you wait until the spring thaw?"

I felt a blush further reddening my already windburned cheeks. I
knew I had chosen a particularly inclement season to come to
Canada. "But I had to," I said.

"Tell me why," July said, slouching down in her huge sealskin
parka until only her nose and eyes were visible. The dogs, still
panting, had bunched together against the icy cold. Numbing gusts
of wind ruffled their gray-and-white neck fur. I changed position.
The fur of my parka touched the fur on July's.

My voice had an odd resonance when I spoke. "A week ago I was
sitting in a beautiful garden in Santa Barbara having tea with a
friend of mine named Cyrena. It was as warm as a summer day."

July's eyes grew wide. "You mean you left warm weather to come
here?"

A burst of wind hit me and it was so cold I could hardly form
words. "I had to see Agnes," I mumbled.

July giggled. "I think you've been seeing too many Indians."

We both had a shivering laugh.

"Listen to what happened," I said. "Each time I reached for my
teacup, a very large monarch butterfly landed on it. At first I was
annoyed. It wasn't going to let me drink my tea."

"Then what happened?" July asked.

"That butterfly kept jumping at me. It landed on my nose and forehead. Cyrena shrieked with laughter. Suddenly it flew away to the north. I pointed at it, and it came back and landed on my finger. It was so beautiful as it clung to me, its large reddish orange-and-black wings folding and unfolding. Its tiny legs seemed to be pulling at me. We stared at each other a long time. Then it flew away due north and disappeared out of sight."

"There aren't any monarch butterflies in the winter," July said.

"I know."

"And I don't think it would fly north at this time of year."

"That's exactly why I had to find out about it."

"Do you think it was a medicine sign?"

"I certainly do. You don't think I'd come 2,500 miles to this deep freeze for anything else!"

July shrugged. "I understand. I wish I'd get a little signal from power telling me to go down to Florida."

We had a hearty laugh and hugged. July got up and cried "Gee, gee!" to the dogs, and we were quickly on our way again. The dogs had regained their spirit and ran diligently ahead of us. It was faster snow because the sun was dropping.

We skirted a mogul of icy snow that glittered like dark crystals in the fading light. As the sun dipped below the horizon the wind suddenly died, and a vast stillness pervaded the white plateau. I became increasingly anxious that nightfall would overtake us before we reached Agnes Whistling Elk's cabin. I was about to express my concern to July when we both saw a tendril of smoke in the distance, snaking up into the twilight.

We elbowed each other and hooted through our chapped lips. My cheeks were too cold to smile. As we approached, the cabin became more distinguishable; it looked like a great pointed snowdrift. We spent the next half hour digging in and, in the semidarkness, fed the hungry dogs slabs of frozen moose meat. We stowed the sled and harness, and staked the dogs for the subzero night. We were in a state of exhaustion and barely uttered a sound.

As we entered the cabin, stamping our icy boots and brushing the snow off our parkas, I realized that Agnes had left a fire going in her stove but she was not at home. With stiff fingers I lit a lantern, and then sat down on a wooden chair in front of the stove. My breath was still steaming because of the coldness, and my cheeks felt wet as they began to thaw. I threw some logs in the stove. Inside the cabin the windows turned blind eyes to the dark wilderness outside. The wind howled and the old cabin logs creaked and growled.

I was joined by July. We sat there numbly, our outstretched hands thrust into the warmth. Neither of us spoke. The radiant heat was wonderfully reviving. I gazed at the flames through the open iron door, and into the glowing belly of the stove. I became aware of a perpendicular shadow on my right against the log wall. With the quickening flames, the shadow swelled and quivered. When I found the source of this curiosity, I had a brief moment of confusion.

"July," I said, alarmed. "That's Red Dog's walking stick, isn't it?"

"Yes, it is," she said in a halting voice. "I can't look at it. It scares me."

"What's it doing here?"

"Who knows," July said, averting her eyes. She was shaking with fear. "I can't help it," she apologized. "He may be near."

For a moment I thought about Red Dog, the sorcerer, a man who had put my life in danger many times. Years ago, he had tried to kill me with that very walking stick. We had been in a life and death struggle over the stolen marriage basket. Because of my apprenticeship to Agnes Whistling Elk, and the skillful training I received from her, I had been able to stalk and return the marriage basket to Agnes, its rightful owner. Now, as always, when I ventured into the far north, there was never a moment that I did not fear the sudden appearance of Red Dog back into my life. I knew he would not rest until he saw me stripped of my power.

"You're thinking about Red Dog, aren't you?" July asked, interrupting the flow of my thoughts.

"Yes, I am."

July touched my hands, her own hand trembling.

"It's okay, July," I said. "Let's take a closer look."

As I approached the walking stick I felt a quiver run up my spine. I realized it was not Red Dog's walking stick after all but only a piece of kindling wood. Was this just a projection of my own fears? Or perhaps Red Dog had been responsible for the illusion. Perhaps he had just wanted to remind us of his presence.

"I think the chill was getting to us," I said to July. "It's only kindling."

I picked it up and handed it to her. She examined it and then suddenly pitched it into the flames, dusting her hands.

"That's what I think of Red Dog," she said.

I looked around and noticed how cozy and different the cabin seemed. A Hudson Bay blanket was draped over the north window, and several caribou hides lay on the bed. Wads of paper had been stuffed in various holes in the walls. The familiar dried herbs and jerky still hung from the rafters. Agnes's medicine shield still hung above her dresser and many red, black, and gray Indian rugs from the south covered the plank floors. As I moved around I became very aware of the noise I made; the snow insulated the cabin and intensified each sound.

I had spent so many happy hours sitting here with Agnes. Never had I arrived that she had not been here with a greeting. And she had always had an interesting story or anecdote to hold my interest as we whiled away the long evenings. There was no way for me to ever contact her. She just somehow always knew I was coming. Her absence affected me deeply. I missed her and was confused about what to do. I had never ventured here in the depths of winter, and I began to wonder if I had made a mistake. I had had such a strong instinct to come, but it was a heavy winter, and everyone—my mother, my daughter, July's family—had warned me against attempting the journey.

"Lynn! Here—look." July had found a note written on a brown paper sack on the sink. Excitedly I held the note by the light of the lantern. It said "Welcome," and that Agnes had been called away on an emergency to Churchill.

"Churchill! That's so far from here! When could she possibly be coming back?" I was alarmed.

"Look at what else she says," July said, pointing to the note. It said that Agnes had known of my coming and had left me a

precious gift in the butterfly tree out in the horse pasture.
"Remember that the flight is forever. Enjoy it, and I will return
when I can. In spirit, Agnes."

July and I awoke at first light in the morning. The windows were
opaque with frost and snow. We made a couple of dashes at the
stove, loading it with wood, and then quickly crawled back in our
sleeping bags. We got dressed inside them and waited for the cabin
to warm up before getting out. July went out to tend to the dogs,
and I started melting snow for water, keeping the fire well stoked.

Over tea and caribou jerky, I read and reread the note that Agnes
had left for me. Anticipation was building inside me. "Come on,
July. I want to see what Agnes has for me at the tree. I wonder why
she left it there. It must be big."

July smiled and gulped her tea. It wasn't long before we had
buckled on our snowshoes and were tromping across the snowdrifts
over to the horse pasture. Our footsteps left great Sasquatch tracks
in the snow. The sun was shining and the snow dazzled our eyes. I
was amazed at how different the area looked. What had been a lush
pasture, teeming with insects, birds, and animals was now deserted.
The terrain was white as far as the eye could see.

We had walked for about fifteen minutes when the butterfly tree
first came into view. It struck me as curious how different it was
now from the last time I had seen it. I had been walking along with
Agnes when I had looked up from our conversation. The sight of
the tree had staggered me. The limbs were entirely covered with
monarch butterflies. The entire tree seemed to expand and contract
with their scintillating movements. There were so many of them
that they obscured even the largest branches from view. It was the
first time I had ever seen this amazing phenomenon.

I had wanted to stay there looking at the butterflies, but Agnes
had insisted that we leave at once. Agnes had said that the tree was
a trickster tree, and that it wanted to steal certain parts of my body.
When I had told her I thought she was trying to scare me, she had
become angry and insisted one of the branches would take my leg at
any moment, and that I would look pretty strange hopping back to
the cabin on one leg. I had laughed at her, but as I was laughing I

had felt a tickling sensation course up my right leg. Agnes had refused to speak about the butterfly tree ever again. But first she had extracted a promise, which I readily gave, that I would never look at the butterfly tree for more than a few minutes without her being present. I had managed to avoid the tree entirely for the rest of my stay.

Looking at the tree now, as July and I made our way across the snowy field, it seemed odd that the leafless old giant had so frightened me. But then, so many strange things had occurred in this north country that defied explanation. My stomach began to tighten.

"July, I don't see anything." There was no visible object waiting for me in the branches of the tree. Ten feet from the tree I began to tremble and become more alert. I saw a gaping hole in the trunk of the tree at about shoulder height.

We walked around the tree several times, kicking at the snow in the chance that the gift had been buried. "Maybe Agnes hid it," July said. "She probably put it inside the trunk."

"Do you think I should look?"

July nodded her head at the hole. "Where else could it be?"

Both of us began kicking snow in a mound to use as a pedestal. July scooped with her snowshoe, using it as a sort of shovel. We were both panting, but were able to build the mound a couple of feet high.

"Why would Agnes put anything way out here in the pasture? Why didn't she just leave it in the cabin?" I asked.

"Who knows why Agnes does anything?" July asked rhetorically.

We both stepped back and again examined the tree. The bark was encrusted with ice and caught dreamlike flickerings of color from the sunlight.

"I guess you're right, July. It must be inside the trunk, unless Agnes forgot to bring it here."

"Agnes never forgets anything," July said.

"You're right. My gift is here somewhere."

I stepped up on the packed snow mound as gracefully as I could, and put my mittened fist into the hole until my arm disappeared up to my elbow. My heart was racing. I felt like a she-bear looking for honey. Tenatively, I felt around inside. The interior of the tree felt rough and seemed to travel down at an abnormal angle. I fumbled around. Space and then more tree. Nothing. I looked at July and shrugged my shoulders.

"Try with your other arm," July said.

I explored inside the tree trunk again, with no more luck than the first time.

"Let's pack more snow and see if you can stick your head down inside and take a look," July suggested.

"I think it's too dark to see anything," I said. "What do you suppose is in there?"

"I don't know," July chuckled. "Maybe it's a bag of gold."

"Never can tell anything for sure with Agnes," I said, nearly slipping as I got down from the mound. "Okay, let's build this thing higher. I'm going to get what's in there if it takes all day."

We both used our snowshoes as digging tools and mounded the snow higher until it was halfway up the trunk to the first branches. Now I was reticent to try again. My stomach tightened even more. But with a flap of my elbows and a few slippery footholds, I scaled the mound and approached the hole from this new vantage point. As I put my mittened hands on either side of the cavity to balance myself, I noticed with surprise that there were worn places at the edges. I scraped the snow away.

"I wonder how old this tree is, July?"

"Very old," she answered. "It's a great-grandmother tree. She must have many children."

The worn places at the edges seemed to be handholds, as if many hands had been there before me. It reminded me of old bones when I touched it, as if the flesh had been stripped away by the long winter, leaving only the essential armature of its body. "Look, July, at how worn this wood is."

July got on the mound with me. We both traced the worn-smooth wood with our mittens. "It looks like this hole has been used for something," July said, shaking her head in wonder.

"Look inside," I said.

"Not me," July said. "You look." She slid off the mound.

I didn't know why I was getting so nervous. This was only an old tree with a big hole in it. I brushed the fur on my hood back from my face and got in a more comfortable position. Slowly I put my head inside the hole. The opening was shaped in such a way that I could barely fit. When I entered the space I had to push slightly, and the edge of the hole rested against my fur collar. There was a sudden tremulous vibration, and the mound of snow I was standing on seemed to drop slightly.

"What's in there, Lynn? What is it?"

I was about to answer July, but all at once I was gone. I felt a weightlessness, as if my body had disappeared. A vacuous darkness was moving toward me, or I was being sucked into it. Then I began to make out a flowerlike shower of sparks; they were flying off in all directions from a center point. I realized I was being propelled by some inward force into this beautiful concentric pattern. My thoughts seemed to retard this process, so I made my mind a blank. The sparks became a great pinwheel that quickly swallowed me.

I was no longer conscious of July or the tree. The whole of my earthly life seemed preternatural. All of time had collapsed and become one-dimensional, a filmy nonsubstance that I was struggling to fracture and go beyond.

I heard a female voice speaking softly. "This is the Spirit House of Butterflies." The words seemed to enfold me and pull me even farther, like a swimmer on a wave.

The fiery point vanished. Standing in a swirling mist was a most beautiful Indian woman. Her long black hair hung down to her moccasins. She was wearing a fringed, beaded doeskin dress and was holding a large, swordlike crystal in her left hand.

"Who are you?" I heard myself ask.

"I am Butterfly Woman. You are on the threshold of the place where the butterflies come from."

"Why have you brought me here?"

"We have drawn you here with our magic songs. You must first climb the butterfly tree to where I live, and then I will reward you."

Suddenly she was gone, and in her place was the butterfly tree as

I had first seen it, its trunk at my feet and its branches obscured by countless fluttering butterflies. It towered into the heavens.

"Climb the tree to the nest at the top," her faint voice called from the distance.

I was mesmerized by the beauty before me. I looked up into the tree branches and caught glimpses of shimmering black and orange satin and tiny sheets of velvety red turning to peacock blue. The tree had taken on another life, a release into its own ecstatic dream —its shape being carried away on fluttering wings. For a moment I was overjoyed.

As I struggled up the tree trunk to the first branch, my being seemed to be weighted down by hundred-pound sacks of sand. The butterflies ignored me. I knew I would never make it to the top. I was so exhausted when I got to the lowest branch that I perched there, leaning against the trunk, and started to fall asleep. A whirring sound startled me awake, and a butterfly just like the one I'd seen in Santa Barbara flew right between my eyes, then up to the next branch. It was frantic, like a dog needing help, and urged me on. I mustered all the will I had and climbed one more branch as if I were being pulled by an invisible cord. I seemed to be dragging a spirit form of my physical body. It was so heavy I felt like I was hauling a buffalo up, branch by branch. At the fourth branch the butterflies made a droning sound as if they were trying to cloud my senses and put me to sleep. The little butterfly flew around me, taunting me, attempting to goad me onward. But I couldn't move. As I started to fall asleep I almost lost my balance, and a great thunderclap sounded in my ears. It scared me so that I leapt to the next branch and then another and another. Each branch had its own demons. The butterflies suddenly transformed themselves into nameless monsters and then became rearing white stallions. Then they were old hags, and then devouring mothers. Then the butterflies held up their polished wings as if they were so many mirrors. As I peered into them I saw a grotesque reflection, the dark side of myself. It was as if the butterflies were trying to terrify me into losing my balance.

Toward the top the little butterfly flew right into a wall of flames

created by the other butterflies rubbing their tiny legs together. He
came out on the other side of the flaming branch unscathed and
transformed for a moment into a rearing white stallion. If it hadn't
been for that courageous little fellow, I would never have ventured
through the blue-hot flames. But I followed and made it to the top,
where a huge nest made out of mud and bizarre pieces of wood was
perched. I climbed over the edge into the nest. It was as if I were
at the top of the world. There stood the beautiful Butterfly Woman
beside a smooth river stone with a hollow place in the top.

"The springs of magic and wet places of power are running dry,"
she said. "Come drink of this clean water from this spring." A jet of
water spouted up from the smooth stone, and I cupped my hands
and drank gratefully.

The butterfly landed on the woman's head, and her long black
hair turned into a fluttering mass of velvety reddish orange-and-black
butterflies. She was so luminescent and breathtaking that I just sat
at her feet.

"Why was I sent here?"

"You have been sent here that you may die by my hand." She
reached out her fingers and I felt a pulling sensation. Then I saw
first my left arm float out into space and then my right.

"These bones that are your body represent the stars. Your head is
the moon and your heart is the sun." She dismembered my body,
each part floating away, until only my spirit remained looking at this
scene. I felt no pain and no fear. Somehow I knew this was
supposed to be. Then she brought the pieces of my body back down
out of the sky and took crystals from the spring beside her. I
watched her open places in my body and insert crystals in my heart,
my head, all over. Then she sewed me back together, my limbs
hanging like those on a rag doll. She picked up a pair of scissors and
cut my hair like a china doll's—straight across the bottom and
straight bangs just above my eyebrows.

"This cut represents the four corners," she said, "the powers of
the four directions." She traced my fingers with hers over the
corners created at the end of the bangs and the front of the longer
hair on the sides.

"In the spirit world you will be seen with this haircut from now on. Your hair is the extension of your spirit. It is your sacred headdress and tells of your medicine journey with the Butterfly Woman. Now we can talk. We can talk of two ways of seeing."

I looked at her wide-eyed, and tears rolled down my cheeks. "Do I have to go back down that tree? Its beauty is deceiving."

"Yes, beauty always has another side. If you look at something carefully, as a medicine woman, you will always be able to see the dark side too. One cannot exist without the other and yet, your people choose never to look into the shadows. They fear the devil. On your climb up the tree, what did you see?"

"I saw horrible things, monsters and fires. When I looked into the mirrors I saw an ugly, hideous reflection of myself. It wasn't really me . . . was it?"

"Yes, it was. But you were brave. You looked at it and chose to leap through it. Later you will realize what a great lesson that was for you. Right now it is good enough that you understand that it is what you choose not to observe in your life that controls your life. That is your lesson here. Do you understand me?"

"I think so."

"If you had looked away from your own reflection, no matter how horrible, you would have fallen from the butterfly tree forever. You would have fallen back into endless sleep. I could not have reached you there. That would have been your tragedy. When men and women fall away from their own vision of sacredness, their culture falls away into sleep with them. Sacred vision contains the balance of light and dark. Here, it's like this." She took two magnetic lodestones and put them together, first the two positive ends, then the two negative ends, and we watched them repel each other. Then she stuck the positive and negative together, and they held in union.

"The positive and negative need each other for creation, for the tourbillion to take place."

"What is the tourbillion?"

"It's like a whirlwind of fire, the source, the primal creation." As she spoke she raised her hands, and a great fiery spiral rose up between us. We watched it spin for several minutes. She came over and placed her hands on either side of my head.

"Look, Lynn, *now*. Look through the crystals in your eyes and see the tourbillion." I felt a subtle shift inside me and I began to look differently at the fiery spiral. I witnessed the elements that made up the fire. They appeared to be male and female energy particles, positive and negative. The female would perform an imploding action and the male would explode. Then the male would implode and the female would explode, pushing and pulling the energy forms in a whirling dance.

"Everything begins with a circle of motion. Without positive and negative poles, there would be no movement, no creation," she said, taking her hands from my head. The fire slowly receded, spinning into the ground.

"Without the dark side, your beauty would not exist. Don't be afraid to look at both sides. You need them both. You must honor all existence as part of the Great Spirit."

I watched her sitting serenely, surrounded by butterflies, and a brooding ache came over me.

"What's the matter?" she asked.

"Will I ever see you again? It's been such an ordeal to get here. I feel such peace here. I would so like to stay and learn from you." I wanted to cry.

"You have already died to who you were. Everything is the same and nothing is the same. Now you truly see. Look with the crystal in your heart. Go ahead, look at me and see your answer for yourself." Suddenly I saw myself as a little girl pleading with my mother not to leave me. I began to sob. In a flash I relived my childhood and saw my fears of being grown up.

"Think of your shields, Lynn. Think of your woman and man shields, and then your little girl and little boy shields. Think of how they represent all the selves within you."

I saw my shields set out in a circle around me. I sat in my little girl shield, crying in the south on the medicine wheel. I stopped crying and moved to the east to my little boy shield. Immediately, I felt like throwing an angry tantrum at my inability to control the situation. Then I felt better.

"Now go to your woman shield in the west," she directed. A new confidence came over me, and I realized the power and wisdom I

was feeling. "Now move to your man shield in the north." It was
there I saw my problem. My sense of responsibility faltered. I
wanted to blame *it* on somebody else, but I didn't even know what
*it* was, or whom to blame but myself.

"You have climbed the butterfly tree, Lynn. Your position of
responsibility in the world has now begun. Do you see?"

I paused for a long moment, not wanting to see. I started to shift
back to my little girl shield, tears welling up in my eyes. Then I saw
what was happening. I may never see the Butterfly Woman again.
The gift had been given, and it was up to me to use it.

"The butterfly is beautiful only for its season. Like a warrioress,
she touches the world briefly with her iridescent wings and then
becomes transformed into another form of life, as will you."

She held her palms over my spirit shape and ran them up and
down about an inch from me. Humming under her breath, she went
to the butterfly tree. She took six cocoons from it, placing many tiny
crystals from the spring inside of them, and turned them into
rattles. She tied them to a six-foot-long stick from the tree and stuck
it in the ground. She sang to me, as she related to the spirit of the
tree, to help heal me of my wounds where the crystals had been
placed.

> You are the spirit woman of words.
> I am mending you,
> curing what hurts you.
> I look in the crystals.
> I will cure you.
> I sew you up,
> I sew you up.
> I hold Mother Bear here.
> I help you fight,
> Great Spirit.
> Thank you for being here.

Her words were simple, but her music was stunningly complex,
celestially beautiful. As she sang she continued to run her hands
over my spirit shape, and the rattles—the crystal-filled cocoons—

agitated up and down the stick without her touching them. When the cocoons would stop moving, she would direct her attention, her healing energy, to that part of my body where her hands were. This continued, and she repeated the song over and over until she seemed satisfied.

Finally she took my hands and led me to the tree. The little butterfly appeared and flew around my head. He seemed happy, as if I were taking him out for a walk. I had to laugh. He seemed filled with anticipation. "He is my ally," she said, smiling at him. "When you see him at times in your life, remember me and know that I am dreaming you and sending you power. Take this branch from the tree and use it to play your drum. Remember the teaching in the butterfly tree and, above all, know that the flight is forever." And she was gone.

I couldn't help but cry as I crawled over the rim of the nest and stepped on the top branch of the tree. She was so wonderful, and I was so afraid of the tree. It wanted to eat me. The butterfly flew down ahead of me as I descended. Again I felt the heavy sensation, although not as badly as before. At every branch there was some terror to face. I went through the fire more easily, and the mirror images in the shining butterfly wings seemed like mere caricatures of the former images. I got to the second branch from the bottom and heard the far-off sound of July's voice saying, "Lynn, come on. Do you see anything?"

I saw that the last branch was being chewed away by hundreds of butterflies. The little butterfly was flying up and down as if to say, hurry, hurry. My body weighed hundreds of pounds and I could barely move. I was so tired and sleepy that I began to dream a beautiful dream about a handsome warrior, but then I struggled with all of my will and reached the lowest branch leaving him behind. I fell the rest of the way down, and the next thing I knew, I was pulling my head out of the hole. I slipped and then slid off the pile of snow on my back, still clutching the branch. July was laughing at me and helped pull me to my feet.

"Is that all Agnes left you? An old stick?"

There is this cave
In the air behind my body
That nobody is going to touch:
A cloister, a silence
Closing around a blossom of fire.
When I stand upright in the wind,
My bones turn to dark emeralds.

James Wright<br>"The Jewel"

# Chapter 2
# The Butterfly Tree

At twilight two weeks after July and I had arrived, to our great joy, Agnes and Ruby returned. Two Inuit men, one Cree man, and three dogsleds came with them. After a night's rest the men continued their journey back to their villages in the west, leaving Agnes and Ruby a sledload of meat for the dogs.

I was relieved to see them go. I watched their sleds disappear from view through bloodshot eyes, sleepless eyes. I had never experienced a night quite like the one that had just passed. I plumped down gingerly on a mogul of snow, groaning—every bone and muscle in my body ached. I had slept on the floor, covered with caribou hides. The Inuit man named Mike had been very large, fat and jovial with a scruffy beard that hung like old Spanish moss from his wide face. He had brought three six-packs of beer that he called "weasel piss." After the fourth can, he had rolled up in my sleeping bag, fallen into a dead sleep, and had not moved for twelve hours. If he had been face down, maybe it wouldn't have been so bad. But he had flailed on his back like a beached walrus and snored outrageously all night. To add to the problem, the other men had consumed equally large quantities of weasel piss and had draped themselves around the cabin in exhausted slumber. The noise from their snoring —a chorus of gulps, gurgles, and choking sounds—had been enough to terrify even the mice, who had hidden in the corners, their tiny eyes shining in the darkness. Ruby and Agnes had been so tired that

they had slept through it, adding a wheezing and whistling harmony
of their own. July and I had lain back to back for warmth, and
neither of us had slept a wink. In the morning the men were very
sheepish when they realized that their own bedding had not been
unrolled. They had great respect for Agnes and Ruby. They cleaned
up the cabin and the Inuit men were gone in an hour.

The Cree man, who lived near July's village, left soon after. He
was to take both his and our dog teams back to July's family and
return for us in one month. I soon realized that the dogs consumed
a huge amount of caribou meat, fish, or whatever could be
scrounged up for them. Feeding these wonderful dogs in the midst
of winter was a real feat.

Agnes and Ruby had been back in the cabin for several days
before it seemed convenient to talk. Their faces were tired and
impassive, and the short days were spent shoveling snow away from
the paths to the shed and smokehouse. Taking advantage of the
brief periods of sunlight, we tried to get ready for the heavy storms
and the rest of the long winter. Darkness fell swiftly, and I found
myself going to sleep at an early hour and having vivid dreams. I
had not spoken of my experience. I held it close to my heart and let
it simmer like a good stew. Once Agnes turned me around while I
was cleaning the stove and gazed deeply into my eyes. She nodded
affirmatively and smiled knowingly, raising her eyebrows.

"I see you got the gift I left for you in the butterfly tree." She
turned abruptly and went outside to gather more wood.

After five or six days I wanted to discuss the butterfly vision with
Agnes. I tried to begin several times, but the moment never seemed
to be right. Living in a confined space with four people, I got into a
certain rhythm. I got accustomed to two inches being enough
private space, and yet I felt a herd instinct. Wolves probably feel
that way in a pack, sensing the frustration or need in the other
members. Agnes sensed my growing hunger to share my experience.
So after a hot meal one windy night, instead of going to bed, she
suggested we all get comfortable around the stove and listen to
whatever I had to tell.

July, Agnes, Ruby, and I sat on the rickety chairs around the fire,
watching the flames leap and dance in the stove. I began to tell of

my ordeal at the butterfly tree. I looked slowly around. The deep
wrinkles on Agnes's and Ruby's faces bled off and became extensions
of the inky black around us. Their faces and July's shone with an
inner light that I have seen only in Indian people in the far north.
Each time I tried to express myself, the words came out sounding
silly. I sat there with hundreds of images clamoring for expression.
Ruby gave out a big belch. Agnes elbowed her and gave her a mock
scathing look.

Ruby glanced at me. "Well, darnit! Did you meet her or not?"

I was sensitive to her sharp manner.

July looked at everyone. "Who?" she asked.

"Yes, I met her," I finally said.

"Well, tell us what she looked like," Ruby demanded.

I cleared my throat and said, "When I first saw her, she had long
black hair to her feet, and she was dressed in a beaded doeskin
dress. She held a crystal in her left hand. The next time I saw her,
she was standing by a spring with crystals in it and her hair turned
into a mass of butterflies. She had an ally with her, a butterfly like
the one I saw in Santa Barbara that brought me here. It acted like a
little dog and then . . ."

July, overcome by the mystery of my incredible reply, said
indignantly, "Wait a minute! Slow down! What woman with
butterfly hair? What butterfly ally? Has the chill gotten to you or
what?"

Agnes and Ruby were guffawing and slapping their knees. July,
who had been looking so serious, began giggling while watching me
in absolute wide-eyed wonder.

Ruby brushed the tears from her eyes and said to July, "You
don't have to be concerned over Lynn's mental health."

"Ho! Wait," Agnes said emotionally, seeing the dejection in my
eyes, and shaking her head at July. "Lynn had a confrontation with
a sovereign being. That being has been waiting for her a long time
in that tree out there. You listen, July. And listen with respect. It's
written on the wind that one day you will meet that spirit of the
forest, maybe pretty soon. Maybe it would be a good idea to be
more tolerant."

There was a long, incubating silence. Ruby drummed her

fingernails on her chair and grumbled, casting her eyes to the rafters. July looked embarrassed and threw some wood on the fire.

"Well, what's the matter with you, Ruby?" Agnes asked.

"I just don't think it's right," she huffed.

Agnes stood up, shoving her chair backward. "What's not right?" she asked, putting her hands on her hips.

"How come your apprentice gets to do all the talking? Lynn talks too much anyway."

"She doesn't."

"Yes, she does. And I don't think it's fair." She turned her face away and pouted like a little girl.

"Ruby, stop it. Lynn wants to explain her experiences while she still can."

"Well, I don't want to hear about it."

"Go take a walk then. There's a nice blizzard brewing outside."

"Very funny. You should have been a clown, Agnes."

"It's okay, Ruby. I'd like to hear about Lynn's encounter," July said, shrugging her shoulder.

"See! Everyone's against me. Even my own apprentice. What next! Every time Lynn shows up around here, there's trouble. It just makes me want to hiss."

"Go ahead and hiss, then," Agnes said.

"I'm leaving." Ruby got up from her chair and started toward her parka.

I caught a mischievous glint in Agnes's eye as she stuck out her boot, tripping Ruby and sending her flying into a heap on the piled caribou hides. Agnes leaped onto Ruby, tickling her. July started tickling me and pushing me. We all fell in a howling, laughing heap of arms and legs. The child's play was just what was needed. After several minutes we got up, put on some coffee, and sat down the way we were before.

"Shall we try again?" Ruby smiled somewhat sheepishly, winking at me.

Sipping my coffee and with my eyes half-closed, I began to tell them the details of the whole incredible experience. It felt so good to express what I had seen—the stew definitely needed to be served.

Every once in a while I would look at July's awestruck expression, but she said nothing. When I had finished, there was a long silence.

"Was the woman Indian?" Ruby asked.

I nodded.

"Are you sure?"

I nodded again.

"When I met Butterfly Woman she was white."

"That's interesting. When I met her she was Chinese," Agnes said.

I looked from Ruby to Agnes, trying to catch a hint as to whether they were pulling my leg. July was staring at all of us. I had just decided they weren't kidding, when Ruby belched and said, "Is there any more of that weasel piss?"

She and Agnes laughed uproariously. We all laughed until our sides ached. Then, as quickly as a shade being drawn, the mood in the room changed to one of seriousness. Agnes changed places with July to sit next to me and Ruby leaned very close. I became absolutely alert and quiet. Agnes looked just past me and said, "Now, Lynn, tell us exactly what you saw from the moment you put your head into the butterfly tree. This time dream with your explanation, and don't miss anything. This is very important."

Again I went through the experience, and, oddly enough, July couldn't seem to keep her eyes open. She curled up on the bed and fell fast asleep. Agnes didn't seem to be too interested in the beginning of my story, but when I started to talk about my climb up the butterfly tree she stopped me for every detail and asked my interpretation.

"How did you feel when you started up the tree?" Agnes asked, peering at me over her nose.

"I felt so heavy, as if I weighed a ton. Why was that?"

"You were carrying the weight of your unresolved lives."

"Unresolved lives?"

"Yes, every thought you think in your lifetime has a life of its own and has a will to live and survive. This is particularly true when your thoughts are unresolved. Thoughts are like people. They have to be buried properly. If a thought is negative or unresolved, it's lurking around for you to finish what you started and bury it in the right way, make it complete. When your thoughts are contradictory, and have no clarity, you create a universe of thought forms that actually live off your energy. And why not? You are their mother in a strange way."

"That doesn't sound good."

"Good or bad? Why do you say that? It's neither. It's simply the way it is. When a medicine woman looks at you she sees what's going on. Most people invite the guests and furnish themselves as the meal. Fears always manifest themselves to the one who creates them. I can see when your spirit is food and what entity is eating you. You have many fears around you, and that is why you are so heavy. Without your food-gift of energy, the entity would waste away and perish."

"What if I don't want to be heavy, don't want to have those suckers around me?" I blurted.

Ruby and Agnes both laughed, but I felt a chill all over.

Ruby said, "We didn't ask you to give birth to those thought entities around you. You chose that circumstance." She turned to Agnes. "You know, sometimes they look like bats flapping all around her."

I said to Agnes in a pleading tone, "Please give me an example."

Agnes laughed. "Ho, I'll give you an easy one. You have had a great fear of death. Is that not true?"

"Yes, I suppose it is."

"That's quite a large entity that you've carried around. It's much better now, but he still watches you constantly. He has a big black mouth and needs to eat. The only thing he can eat to live is you. That's one of the entities that can completely devour you."

"Nobody wants to die," I said defensively.

Ruby cut in. "Every time you think, 'I'm afraid to die,' you give that ugly, drooling entity a tenderloin venison steak." She laughed like a hag. "Yeah, you give 'em one of those big crawfish and some of that 'Pierre' water you drink." She was making fun of what I had said in an earlier conversation when I had described dining on lobster at a lavish restaurant in Los Angeles.

"That's right," Agnes continued. "No one wants to die and neither does your fear of death."

I stared at the two women for a moment and then looked at my hands. I was getting angry, especially at Ruby. But I knew they were right.

"When you have a negative thought, it steals your life force to some degree. Haven't you ever wondered why you get tired and depressed when you think about certain things?"

"No. I've never thought about it."

"It's because you've created a parasite, like mistletoe, which lives off another life source—you. Because of that, it has the potential to kill you."

I locked eyes for a moment with Agnes and then looked away. "OK, I see. So what do I do to get rid of it?"

"You shake the entity off your trail in this case by understanding your fear of death. You did that in the tree. Make death an ally instead of an enemy. Then your fear thought form goes off and dies."

"Oh. It's kind of like saying that the only way out is in."

"Lynn, it's very simple. Take responsibility for your thoughts and the beings they create. That's all."

For some reason I felt Agnes and Ruby were forcing their ideas on me rather than waiting for me to grasp them in my own time. I was getting defensive and angry. Rarely did I feel like I was being lectured, but I did now. Then I remembered Zoila Guiterez, a shamaness I had met in the Yucatán. She had described my addictions to me. Agnes and Ruby were still chuckling.

"Wait a minute," I said. "That's what Zoila said about my fears being a prop."

Agnes smiled and patted my knee. "That's right."

"Well," Ruby huffed. "Are you ever going to tell me about this Zoila and your trip to the Yucatán, or are you going to completely leave me out after all I've done for you?"

"So much happened to us down there. I'll try to compose my thoughts and tell you what happened tomorrow night."

Ruby pouted. "Is that a promise?"

"I promise." Agnes and I both laughed.

"Back to the tree, Lynn. Tell us what happened on the second branch."

"I started to fall asleep. I couldn't keep my eyes open. Isn't that odd?"

"No, it was your own psychic sleep catching up with you. It was a reflection of all the times you've snoozed instead of staying aware. It almost got you."

"It would have if it hadn't been for Butterfly Woman's ally, the butterfly."

"So he helped you. That's a good sign."

"Why?"

"Because he will always be a lifeline for you."

"That's funny. During the climb up the tree, it was as if I were hanging onto an invisible cord."

Agnes and Ruby nodded in satisfaction, looking at each other momentarily.

"That cord lives in your will. The butterfly helped you sense it. You will learn how to throw it out ahead of you in times of danger and follow it to safety at the end. Now go on."

"When I started to sleep, I almost fell."

"Ho. You see your fear of death saved you that time. In this case, fear was an ally."

"I climbed up several big branches covered with butterflies who had highly polished wings, reflecting so many horrible aspects of Crazy Woman."

"What Crazy Woman?" Ruby stamped her foot. "There you go again! You wouldn't be leaving me out if I weren't blind."

"Ruby, shush. Tomorrow night we will speak of Lynn's journey to the Yucatán. Now either pay attention, or butt out of this conversation."

"Humph. You're always making me wait just to get my goat."

Agnes frowned. "Go ahead, Lynn. Ignore Ruby."

I paused, but Ruby didn't say anything more. She merely glanced upward and left her gaze there, as if she were bored to tears.

"Well, I suppose I came face-to-face with my own ugliness," I said.

"And . . . ?"

"Agnes, the training I received in the Yucatán from Zoila has served me well. I understand the value of the devouring side of myself for the first time."

"Good," Agnes said, saluting from her midsection. She gave me a quick hug like that of a school chum's.

"There were rearing horses in the polished wings, stallions."

Ruby, still looking up at the ceiling, asked, "What color?"

"White."

She leaned forward to look at me with her head cocked. "Hmmm." She pursed her lips, giving them a fluted look like delicate pie crust. "White, yes."

"What do you think, Ruby?" Agnes asked.

"It might well be," she said.

"Maybe," Agnes said. "I think so."

I looked impatiently from Agnes to Ruby. "What? What?"

"Dreamer medicine," Agnes said.

"Later, later," Ruby said, waving her hand. "Isn't it fun to be left out? Chew on it and see what it tastes like."

I fumed. "Oh, well," I said. "I'm not interested anyway. As I was saying before Ruby interrupted me, next and last on the tree was a branch of fire. The butterfly flew right through it and I followed, terrified. But I followed. The fire was an enormous wall that lashed convulsively in every direction. Everything was on fire." I waved my arms expansively to make Agnes aware of the dimensions of the fiery branch. She was silent but nodded her head.

"It was my fear of death again, wasn't it?"

"Yes, my daughter. This fear may one day overtake you. Until you make death your ally, you will blunder and make many mistakes. It could paralyze your existence and make you helpless."

Ruby clapped her gnarled old hands together. "So was there a cute little nest at the top?"

"Yes, it was strange and marvelous."

Ruby stood up. "Oh, really, dearie. Was it simply marvelous?" She threw her shoulder back extravagantly, and, limp wrists and all, sauntered around her chair. "Simply, simply."

I couldn't help but laugh at Ruby and her antics.

She went over to the bed near July, and whispered something in her ear. July stirred in her sleep and then sat bolt upright. She rubbed her eyes and said, "What did I miss?"

"You missed very little," Ruby said.

"Let's have some tea." Agnes headed for the teapot and crumbled some herbs into the steaming water. After it had steeped for several minutes, she poured it through a cloth into four cups. Sipping my tea, I remembered the difficulty I had had descending from the tree.

"Agnes, when I was climbing down, at the second-to-last branch I got sleepy again and terribly heavy. The little butterfly got very nervous. A very handsome, young, hero-like man appeared before me and beckoned. He was so handsome. I'll never forget his face." I was soon lost in a reverie, dreamily remembering him. I had instantly fallen in love.

"What?" July asked, an eagerness in her voice. "You met a man in a tree around here? And you say he was very handsome?"

"July, go back to sleep," Agnes said.

July took a deep breath, resigned to her confusion.

"I remember that the branch below me was being gnawed away by hundreds of butterflies. I realized that if I stayed with him, my chance to find safety would be gone forever. I hesitated and nearly didn't make it. But I climbed down before the branch fell." I tried to convey my feelings in the look I gave Agnes. "I loved him. Why couldn't I have stayed with him?"

"It would have been a quick and painless death, if that's what you mean," she sighed.

"Sounds good to me," July said. "Is he still up there?"

"Humph," Ruby said.

"He had such a beautiful smile," I said. "I can still see him." I leaned back in the chair and went limp. I was beginning to get melancholy.

Agnes jerked her thumb at me, pointing. "Look at her." She shook her head. "When women fall in love, they want to give away their power. You had a choice. Go with him or take your power. What do you think he wanted you to do?"

"He wanted me to go with him."

Ruby snorted. "Wrong!"

"Wrong, indeed," Agnes said. "Look, Lynn, we all come into this earth walk to heal our femaleness. Man or woman, it makes no difference. Women come into this round knowing a great truth. But like most women, you couldn't define what you knew. Some women become indifferent to this knowledge. You wanted to understand this knowledge. This is what brought you here. You found me to help you. When men come into this round, they do not *know*. If they are lucky, they realize they have to find a woman to teach them. Men do not know how to live. Women must teach them that. But first women have to take their own power and heal themselves. They imitate men like a mockingbird imitates a crow. Once they do that, it's all over. It's all wrong. Men and women both lose and become weak. If you had chosen that man, beautiful as he was, and not your own power, he would have destroyed you. He would have hated you for not being White Buffalo Woman for him to learn from. When you are a goddess, then you can mate with your god successfully, and only then."

"Ho!" Ruby said, patting Agnes and me on the back. "July hasn't even seen the treacherous bastard, and she's ready to follow him to her doom."

I was so relieved to have been able to talk about my journey that I fell asleep almost instantly after I had washed my teacup.

Guard the Mysteries!
Constantly reveal Them!

—Lew Welch
"Theology"

# Chapter 3
# Dream Journey to the South

Late in the afternoon a terrible storm came bellowing down off the northern plateaus, blowing icy cold drafts through the chinks in the logs. At times it blew so hard that the crumpled-up wads of newspaper wedged in the tiny cracks would squeak and fly into the room. We all wore layers of long johns and ate mostly in silence, each of us feeling both the vulnerability of our little cabin and the closeness and security of our friendship. The tension and strain was enormous, and the proximity of the four of us forced each one's thoughts into more imaginative realms. I was beginning to understand how years of this kind of stress could lead to visions of the dreaded windigo—the vision that obsessed the spirit of a person, turning the heart to ice and spurring him or her to murder whole villages of people. The windigo is that part inside a person that is mad and can turn to cannibalism of another like being or of oneself. I shuddered to think of that depth of pain and settled myself near the stove with my warmly clad feet propped up on an old wooden apple crate.

"How about some talk of warmer weather?" Agnes suggested.

I could tell that she too was feeling strain from the unceasing cold. Even if I had wanted to leave, there was no way out. Only with my flights of spirit could I deal with my claustrophobia. I watched Ruby, trying to understand her, a proud old woman who held such great power in her mind but who had eyes that saw nothing. She always did everything well: every dish that was cleaned, every blanket that was rolled was done to perfection. Her movements were always calculated, no doubt from her blindness, but also, I sensed, from her great reverence for life and the universe around her. It was a lesson for me just to watch her go through her day. I wondered at her coyote-like gracefulness and her ability to become the knowledge that she wanted me to learn. If I were too serious, she would catch me off-guard by playing the senile old lady or the petulant child. I had never before had the honor to spend this much time so close to her. I was amazed at how separate she remained, always holding her place. And yet I felt so much love for her at the same time.

Agnes scooted a chair over across from me, July pulled up a chair on my left, and Ruby pulled up a chair on my right. No matter how well I knew Ruby, her close presence always made me a little nervous. I never knew what she would do next. I watched her out of the corner of my eye, and I could see her smiling to herself as she picked up the moccasin she had been working on and rubbed it with her hands.

"Lynn, it's time for a good story," Agnes said, a tray of beads in her lap. She picked up some tiny white ones on the point of a needle and went to work on a pouch.

"I agree," Ruby said. "A good story warms the heart."

July said, "I want to hear more about the beautiful man in the tree."

"I said a good story," Ruby snapped. "She is going to tell us of the time she spent in the Yucatán, where it's warm and sunny."

"There's so much to tell. Where should I begin?"

"How about at the beginning!" snorted Ruby.

July giggled.

"OK. Imagine my house . . ."

A fine rain was falling and I could see the threadlike drops through my French windows as I sat in my living room. I was reading the travel section of the Sunday newspaper, noting the bargain flights to Mérida, Mexico, in the Yucatán penninsula. Agnes

had told me about a woman who lived there who, she said, knew a
lot about masks.

"What do you mean? Carved masks?" I had asked Agnes.

Agnes had said that the woman knew about power masks, and
that she had information that predated Mayan civilization. She had
piqued my interest, so I had jotted down the woman's name in my
notebook along with a vague description of the house in the small
village where she lived. Agnes had never mentioned the woman
again, nor had I thought about the conversation until this moment.

I called the airline number in the newspaper advertisement and
made a reservation. It made absolutely no sense from a rational
perspective. For the next three hours I canceled dinner dates,
appointments, autograph parties at bookstores, and all the other
activities I had scheduled. The responses ranged from mild
disappointment to rebuffs to rage. It wasn't my intention to irk so
many people, but I had been working so hard that I felt I deserved
a vacation. Good excuse or not, I was going.

The flight was uneventful. I rented a car at the airport and, with
maps in hand, I drove to the ancient Mayan ruins of Uxmal, and
from there to the small village of 'Llano', which had dirt streets and
adobe houses. Using the smattering of Spanish I knew, I asked a boy
directions to the home of Zoila Guiterez. After much gesturing and
pointing, I discovered that it was a small adobe house set off from
the main village, near a small stream. I thanked the boy, who was
Zoila's grandson, and drove to the house. The yard was small and
well kept. A fetish was tacked in the center of the old wooden door.
I knocked. The door opened and Agnes Whistling Elk was standing
there with a wide grin on her face.

"I was about to give up on you," she said. "I've been expecting
you for three days. Why didn't you come sooner?"

We hugged. I was completely astonished. "Agnes," I said, "I
didn't even know I was coming until yesterday afternoon."

"I was just talking about you with Zoila. Were your ears itching?"

I laughed and said, "You're the last person I expected to see
outside of Canada."

"Oh, you know how it is. We Indians get the itch to smell

around. We follow our noses. Come on in. We were just doing your favorite thing—having tea."

I followed her through the house and into a beautiful garden surrounded by a wooden coyote fence. Sitting on a hand-hewn bench was an elderly woman dressed in a loose blouse or *huipile* and a blue wraparound skirt. She wore leather sandals like most other Indian woman from the Yucatán. Agnes introduced us.

"Didn't I just say Lynn Andrews would knock on the door soon?" Agnes said.

"That you did, Agnes," Zoila said with a slight accent, looking at me. "We've met before in the North, but you probably don't remember me."

I felt an immediate kinship with this remarkable woman. "No, I don't remember. Where?"

"It doesn't matter," she said.

"I'll go get Lynn some tea," Agnes said, smiling. "And don't let her pester you about masks and Mayan lore."

I stood there awkwardly for a moment. "Are you Mayan?" I finally asked.

"I am Mayan," she said. And then she added, "But some people say I'm half bobcat."

I was about to ask her about the masks when Agnes returned with a gourd cup filled with a slightly bitter herb tea. We all sat down. No one said anything as we sipped our tea. I was still confused by finding Agnes at this house. My mind was racing with dozens of scenerios that could explain how Agnes could possibly be sitting in front of me.

Zoila smiled warmly at me. Her eyes were very kind and sweet, but in the shadows I could see a coiled rattlesnake. I knew I should never cross this woman. Her eyes moved across my face, back and forth, as if she were reading my thoughts. Several small children came running into the backyard, and in a high voice a girl asked something of Zoila in Mayan. Zoila answered, and the children stood in a ring around us expectantly. Zoila explained that the children wanted Agnes to tell them another story. Agnes spoke to the children in Mayan. Then she spoke to the girl who had spoken

to Zoila. The little girl ran inside the house and quickly returned
with a teapot. She poured tea in all our cups.

"That one is my granddaughter," Zoila said.

"She's certainly pretty," I remarked.

Agnes excused herself and sat down nearby on the ground. The
children surrounded her in a circle, laughing and crying out
excitedly. A hush came over them as soon as Agnes began her
narrative.

I took the opportunity to say to Zoila, "Agnes said you know
about masks."

"Come over here and sit with me, so we won't disturb the
children," she said.

We went to a corner of the garden and sat on the ground. The
strong aroma of damp earth and subjungle foliage wet from a late
afternoon shower was rich and fertile. I took another sip of tea. This
vantage point enabled me to see through a break in the coyote
fence. In the distance buzzards covered the branches of a dead tree
behind a thatched roof hut.

"Has something died?"

"Oh, no. The buzzards always come and wait for the scraps from
the cantina."

Zoila regarded me for a moment in silence. With the palms of
her hands she smoothed the surface of the ground. She picked up a
thin twig and drew a design in the earth. It was a rectangular
section divided into triangles.

"What does it mean?" I asked.

"It means power, which means a way into understanding
yourself."

"Power. The design has many implications, but how does it mean
power?"

"We call this design a mask of the earth. This mask is our altar.
This is how we pray and arrange our sacredness."

I got my shoulder bag and took out a white shawl that I had
brought for her. I presented it with respect. She examined it and set
it aside with a nod.

"Teach me," I said.

"You have been attracted here as a bee is to a blossom. One of
the reasons you are here is to learn. I will teach you. This evening
you must rest from your long journey. We must siesta now and wait
for knowledge. When you are ready to receive her, knowledge will
arrive. She is a wanderer but never so far away you cannot entice
her into your presence."

As Zoila spoke, a beautiful green hummingbird flew between us
and explored a fuschia bush. Zoila continued, nodding toward our
guest, "Watch how the hummingbird hovers in front of the flower.
Pollen is power to that tiny bird. See, she waits until just the right
moment and then joins with it. She takes what she needs and flies
away."

Practically on cue, the hummingbird moved backward from the
fuschia flower and sped off above the coyote fence. "When power
comes to you, be still with her. Don't discuss it and bleed the
energy away. Just hold it. Slowly she will begin to dance with you,
but only if you are patient and listen for her voice."

Zoila took both my hands and touched them to her heart. My
own heart swelled. We stood up and went over to Agnes and the
children. She was still telling her story, and the children were gazing
at her with rapt attentiveness. The story must have been funny,
because the children laughed delightedly at various points. I
remembered that July had once told me that Agnes spoke ten
Indian languages.

Agnes dismissed the children, and they all scampered away. The
children in their bright clothing of red, yellow, and black made a
charming picture as they ran out the coyote fence. The three of us
walked to where my red Ford was parked. I had rented it only a few
hours earlier, but it seemed like days had passed.

"I'll take Lynn with me, and we'll see you later," Agnes said.

"I'll be there," Zoila said.

Agnes pressed something small into Zoila's hand and winked at
her. We drove down a twisting dirt road that skirted the verdant
jungle, Agnes pointing and giving directions.

"Where are we going?" I asked.

"We are going to visit some friends. There we can rest and eat."

By now I was driving through low jungle on a narrow two-lane road. I sensed we were near the ancient ruins at Uxmal. I thought about Zoila, and I was filled with nervous anticipation at the thought of learning from her. The road seemed to be getting narrower, and the tangled vines and flowers were within touching distance from the car window. "How much farther?" I asked.

"Not far," Agnes answered.

A slight rain was beginning, a fine mist. Beads of water gathered on the windshield, and I switched on the wipers. The road was damp and more dangerous. All I needed was to get stuck in a quagmire in the middle of the jungle. The road cut east and came to a clearing. Moments later we were in the courtyard of a long adobe hacienda.

"Park there," Agnes said.

I noticed that many other cars, jeeps, a camper, and a pickup were parked there in a row. The rain stopped just as we got out of the car.

"Bring your things," Agnes said.

I got the two bags I brought and followed her. The hacienda was surrounded by a glade of jacaranda trees. Great flowering vines hung over the balconies, and our feet slipped on the highly polished tiles as we entered a wide, hand-hewn mahogany door.

"What is this place, Agnes?"

"You are welcome here, as am I. That's all you need to know for now." She came to a stop. "I think you will find your stay here more than you bargained for."

I smiled at the sly gleam in Agnes's eyes. She turned right, and we passed some high-ceilinged, open-air rooms. Outside, the rain began to pelt down. The staccato sound of the large drops blunted the dense bird and insect sounds of the Yucatán. Agnes led on. We went up some stairs to a large room on the second floor. Two beds were in the room, and a row of narrow windows overlooked a courtyard that had a small swimming pool surrounded by squat palm trees. A few women sat on wooden chairs on the veranda, watching the rain and sipping pink drinks in tall glasses with straws.

I put my bags down and opened the horizontal wood shutters.

The lulling, slapping sound of the rain was pleasant and made me drowsy. I wanted a bath and a nap. Agnes had already fallen on her bed and had turned her face into the pillow. Her rhythmic breathing told me she was sound asleep.

After my bath I lay down with great relief on the small, hard bed and watched the fan slowly turning above me. But exhaustion didn't prevent my heart from pounding with excitement, and I was unable to close my eyes. I dressed and quietly left the room. Outside on the portal I sat in a lounge chair and watched the silvery streaks of rain fall steadily. In the distance to the east, lightning split the sky. The women I had seen had vanished, and no one was around. I assumed everyone was taking a siesta.

I felt as if I were in the navel of an ancient civilization. The energy of the Yucatán felt naked, as if thousands of years of life had worn away the usual veils a country wears to protect itself. It seemed as if the Yucatán stood nude before me. Her jungle and rain and foliage weren't hiding from me. She pulsed and stretched out in all directions, flat yet muscular, powerful yet subtle in her strength. She met me in the heart and solar plexus, breath for breath, movement for movement. I was in a great power spot, and all the while I watched, a sea of rain shimmered over the land.

I dozed off and was awakened by Agnes shaking my shoulder. Zoila was with her, both of them dressed festively. The rain had stopped, and the hour was late. Colorful lights lit up the patio, and I could hear women laughing somewhere off in the shadows.

"Is Lynn always sleeping, Agnes?" Zoila asked, lifting a dark eyebrow and peering at me. If the question hadn't come from a medicine woman, it would have seemed harmless. But it sounded like a challenge to me, like something Ruby might say. My back stiffened, and I forced myself awake.

"I hope you're hungry," Agnes said.

"Yes, very," I answered.

Agnes rubbed my back and giggled at me on the way downstairs. She elbowed me like a schoolgirl.

"Relax," she whispered in my ear. "You're too sensitive."

"What is this place, Agnes? Is it some kind of retreat?"

"I believe this is a dining room."

And so it was, a large room with 11 tables and young Mayan women in white flowered dresses serving dinner. There were nine women still eating or having coffee. The three of us sat down, and a young woman brought us all salads, platters of fish, bowls of black beans and rice, and dishes of fried bananas and tropical fruit.

After we ate, Zoila asked me to go for a walk with her in the garden. Agnes returned to the room. A balmy perfume was in the air, and the grounds were full of tropical palms and flowering vines. Zoila took my hand and walked me in the direction of the stairs. She said nothing. The sounds of the female voices seemed to fade, and the night noises began to magnify and crescendo. When she let go of my hand, the chatter of voices returned, louder than the night voices.

"Did you hear that?" I asked, wide-eyed.

Zoila looked at me. "What?"

"The night . . ."

"No, the leaves," she interrupted.

"The leaves?"

"Yes, they spoke to you." Zoila held up her palms to me. "I work with the plants. I use them to heal. I go out at night for various sacred herbs during certain phases of the moon." She took my hand again; it felt hot. She squeezed my hand and then released it. "Listen," she said. "Close your eyes."

I could hear a shift in the sounds, a very faint wailing. I jumped a little and spun around on one foot in a short dance. I came close to falling and then opened my eyes. The rubber plants loomed over me and the earth undulated in heat waves. I sat down on the ground and stared up at Zoila.

"Don't be frightened. Within each of us there is a being that we must come to know. That spirit in you talks to the plant spirits."

I felt giddy.

"Have you never noticed?"

"I have always loved the wind in the trees."

"Close your eyes again, and listen with your heart."

I did so and heard a soft wailing, almost like a woman crying.

Zoila touched my shoulder. "Open your eyes now. You heard her, didn't you?"

"Yes. Who is she?"

"She is *ashana*. I call her the "monkey root" in your tongue. She is a plant and she offers her protection to you. You need her."

"Why do you call her monkey root?"

"She is telling you how she sees you, like monkeys often do when they imitate people. She is very powerful. When you come to stay with me, we will go out and find her together." Zoila gave me a wide grin, turned, and disappeared into the night shadows.

I reoriented myself. The hacienda seemed deserted. I walked quickly upstairs to the room, and found Agnes sound asleep. I couldn't imagine how she could fall asleep so quickly and easily in this remarkable place. I looked at the clock. It was two in the morning! I had been with Zoila for five hours, but it had seemed like only a few minutes.

The next morning I awoke feeling tired. I lay in bed listening to the rain and the din of birds and insects in the dense foliage all around the hacienda. Agnes come out of the bathroom.

"I can't get used to all this civilized living." She indicated the bathroom. "It's not right." She came and sat on the edge of my bed.

"Agnes, I had an incredible experience with Zoila last night." My tiredness disappeared as I spoke.

"Tell me."

"We were walking in the garden. We stopped to listen, and I heard the leaves speaking to me. Also, a root called *ashana* called to me. She sounded like a woman crying."

"*Ashana*. I've heard of her. She keeps away evil spirits. I know a little about that."

"I should have known that you knew about this plant."

"Yes, well, Zoila will be a good teacher for you. She knows the sacred plants of this circle better than anyone."

"It thrilled me to hear the sounds from the leaves. Zoila helped me. The sounds took me, and I danced."

Agnes, watching me as I bounced excitedly out of bed and got dressed, said, "In the old days we always sent an apprentice to another medicine person if she needed to learn powers that were from a different path. Zoila is extremely knowledgeable about plants, but her knowledge is from a different path. I honor her, and I give you to her to learn some of that wisdom."

"I like Zoila," I remarked on the way downstairs.

Agnes and I ate breakfast in the small dining room and then walked over to the ruins of Uxmal. We meandered with delight through the ancient city. Uxmal has a voluptuous, female quality. We would find the magnetic spots in the architectural design that were like acupressure points on a human body and stand on them, breathing in the energy through the soles of our feet. In the afternoon we walked back to the hacienda to take a siesta. I was very aware of my intense love and respect for Agnes as my friend and my teacher. I was also very aware of the similarity in the energy between us, reflected back to us by the Yucatán. We were discovering the magical sights, smells, sounds, and culture of Uxmal together. We were both strangers in this foreign land, and for the first time we were equal, enjoying the experience of something new. Or so I thought.

Agnes left the room after our siesta. While she was gone Zoila's grandson, the one who had given me directions in the village, delivered a note. It said Agnes would not return for dinner, and to wait until the moon was up before following the map on the note.

She comes in through the night walls.
Her music . . . my blood.
Ravenous outpouring,
subtle
as letting go of a hand.

Jack Crimmins
"The Final Mother"

# Chapter 4
# The Final Mother

The jungle was wild with the night cries of birds and animals as I left the hacienda. The dense trees and low brush swayed and creaked in the warm wind. An occasional vine writhed snakelike across my path. Carefully I followed the directions Zoila had sent me. It was growing late. The path led straight through the jungle, which smelled of rotting wood and damp earth. As I walked, I heard the intermittent rustle of leaves. A beast howled and sent a shiver through me. Suddenly I was in front of a crumbling Mayan building, a flat temple with high stone serpents and terraces on either side. The full moon shimmered on the cieba trees and cast an unusual glow. I heard another sound and looked in that direction. Everything became quiet. I went on as the map indicated and entered a dark archway.

Beyond the entrance arch was an immediate turn to the left. Out of the shadows stepped two Amazon-looking women.

"What? Who are you?" I yelled in surprise.

"Do not be alarmed," one of the tall women said, speaking English with a heavy Mayan accent. "We are the appointed guardians of this temple. We are the night walkers who will guide you to your destination. This is a secret place, and you must wear a hood."

She had no sooner said this than the other one put the hood over my head. "Come," she said after fastening it. "Take hold of our arms."

We walked for several minutes. I could smell copal smoke, the incense made from the copal tree. Through the opaque material covering my face I could make out a flickering light. Then I sensed that people other than my escorts were near me.

I was gently pushed down to a sitting position on a cold, hard seat with no back. I touched the smooth stone with my hands and felt rounded carved designs underneath it and along the sides. Then the hood was whisked off, and the guards disappeared into the shadows.

I had tried to keep myself oriented, and I thought I was facing east. I caught my breath. I was sitting in a room with three masked beings. They looked like huge Mayan spirit dolls or kachinas. One was directly in front of me, one on my right, and one on my left. I turned and saw there was a fourth, directly behind me. Each was totally different. The beings across from each other were completely opposite in nature. They were all female, and they seemed to be focused on me. We were enthroned in a square room, all stone, with a vaulted ceiling and no windows. The ambience was ancient, as if we were back thousands of years in time. Several burning torches made the masked creatures and their vibrant colors even more mysterious. The flames undulated and licked at the shadows.

The woman facing me began to move. She was beautiful in the pale firelight. Graceful and sylphlike, she wore a headdress made of gold interspersed with what looked like macaw feathers. A hummingbird was at the crown. I heard music from some unseen place, and she began to hum in a high soprano voice. A drum began a heartbeat rhythm, and a clay flute trilled. Other percussive instruments that I didn't recognize joined in. The masked creature leapt into the air, her skirts swirling, rustling, and quivering around her painted legs. She was wearing twenty or thirty tiers of grass, all painted with shimmering rainbows. Her face was painted exquisitely in rainbow colors, and her long hair was silvery, like Christmas tinsel. She nodded for me to follow and offered me a jade tablet covered in symbols I recognized as Mayan. When I didn't move she

came closer, extending the tablet. Light emanated from her body
like frost sparkling in the sun. She moved to the beat of the music
in imaginative and stylized steps. She danced wildly and expressively
and then stopped and stood in midstride like a pantomime.

I felt a dark energy coming from the being or monster behind
me. She let out a bloodcurdling shriek.

"Look at me!" she screamed.

I turned around, still sitting, to face her. She whirled in spirals of
smoke and her face was a misshapen skull. She had a black band
painted across her vacant eyes. As her bony face inched closer to
me, I could see her serrated teeth. She looked like a mask of death.
She was bald like the north wind or a dead sun. Her hands were like
bird talons. The music became discordant, and the beat pulsed faster
and faster. She whirled until she fell to the stone floor. Dead snakes,
birds, and iguanas hung from her belt, and they now fanned out
grotesquely around her.

A fit or seizure overtook her; it was as if she were possessed by
the worst kind of devils. She raved and moaned and frothed at the
mouth. I rose from my seat and stepped up on the stone chair,
fearing that in her hysteria she might harm me. She slowed, stood
up, and smiled with venomous power. Her broken, black teeth were
threatening. She pulled a skull from beneath her thorn-covered skirts
and bore a black stone knife in the other hand. She sang in a high,
sing-song voice that rang with madness.

> Cut off your hand.
> Cut off your foot.
> Tie you to the floor.
> Stake you to the tree.
> You will never leave me.

When she finished her song, she made a vicious lunge at me. I
recoiled and nearly fell from the chair where I was tottering. I was
so paralyzed with fear, I could hardly move.

"Wait! She's mine," said the woman on my right in a voice filled
with love and compassion. I turned and she danced in front of me,
offering me presents of abundance—fruits, grains, and corn. She

wore a dress of shiny corn silk that shimmered in the torchlight like
summer rain. Her right breast was bare, and it appeared as though
she were suckling a cornhusk baby that was strapped to her. She laid
a basket of cornmeal at my feet. Then, humming a lullaby, she
dusted some cornmeal over my head. Her green hair was layered
with spotted eagle wing feathers. Seven snakes encircled her waist.
Her face was painted yellow, with two red bands running laterally
across her cheeks and nose. She was large and imposing, and moved
with the strength of Mother Earth herself. She swayed right and left
to the drumbeat and motioned for me to follow her. Then she
stopped.

From behind me I heard a dreadful sound that could only have
come from the snout of a pig. I turned to face this new monstrosity.
She carried an armload of snakes, and large furry spiders crawled
over her robe, which was fashioned of dead snakes. Her misshapen
face looked like a mass of gnarled river roots. She was as hideous as
the other being was beautiful. She wore a dress of raven wings that
hung with buzzard claws. Her headdress was fashioned out of gold
and black serpents. As she danced, she threw long, quivering
shadows. She was the personification of all that is baneful, a fiend.
She dropped to the floor, groaning, and crawled toward me. I was
filled with revulsion and terror. She released the snakes at my feet
and looked up at me with pale reptilian eyes. I screamed and lept
backward off the stone chair.

The beings all came toward me, pulling at me and caressing me. I
pushed through them, saw a passageway, and ran for it. They
pursued me as I ran. I was confused and lost and prayed to get out
of there. I tried several passageways, but they all seemed to lead
back into themselves.

Then I saw a light in one of the passages, and I headed for it.
The moonlight led me out an exit. Breathless and with tears
streaming down my face, I saw Agnes and Zoila waiting for me
outside the temple.

"My God, how could you have done this, Zoila?"

"You have experienced an initiation that is as old as time. You
don't know it, but you have passed the test. All that remains is for
you to understand your experiences."

I followed Agnes and Zoila through the jungle trail back to the
hacienda. I was shivering and silent. It seemed strangely deserted
when we arrived. They led me to a small room with hand-carved
furniture, and we sat down.

"What was that all about, Zoila?" I asked.

"What do you think?"

"I think you sent me into a den of monsters."

"No, not monsters. Matriarchs."

"They didn't look like matriarchs to me."

"Do you want to learn, or do you want to argue?" Agnes said.
"Lay your notions down."

"Tell me," I said.

"No," Zoila said. "You tell us. Everything. Omit nothing."

I went through my experiences in the temple, telling everything I
could remember. When I asked a question, I was told to continue
with my narrative. "Please explain these things," I said when I had
finished. "What kind of initiation was it?"

"*La Ultima Madre.* In English it would be called the initiation of
the Final Mother. Each of those women represented a hoop of
energy. In ancient times this ceremony was done by the great
priestesses for the benefit of all pregnant women and initiates. It was
to teach them of themselves and their future children. After their
initiation as la Ultima Madre, they knew who they were for the first
time. They knew why they behaved in a certain manner. Let's look
and see if we can unravel your experiences."

"What kind of energy hoop, Zoila? I was frightened out of my
wits."

"The power of la Ultima Madre is terrifying only if
misunderstood. The first woman that you saw directly in front of
you was the woman of the east. Let us call her Rainbow Mother. To
my people she is Xochiquetzul, the moon goddess. Rainbow Mother
is the energy of the poet, dancer, weaver, and seer. She is the
goddess of marriages and harlots. Artists are intimate with her; she is
their muse. And she is completely misunderstood in your society.
Your people may even attempt to kill her or put her in a mental
institution. Your world does not support its writers and thinkers, so
she is seen as a misfit, a person on the fringes. If she marries she

doesn't nurture her children, she inspires them. Routine wilts her. She is on one end of an arrow.

"On the opposite end is the woman of the west, Crazy Woman or Ilamatecuhtli, goddess of death. Think of her as the dying sun. She was the second woman who enticed you. Some people call her Cannibal Woman."

"Is she like the medusa, whoever looks upon her turns to stone?" I asked, explaining the myth of the medusa to Zoila.

Zoila nodded her head. "Yes, she would turn you to stone and strip you of all your sacredness. She does not wish to kill you, but to maim your talents and paralyze your ability. You know of the mad poet or insane artist. It's because of Crazy Woman. She always pulls on your sanity and tests you. She tries to lure you across the crossroads."

"Where is that?"

"You were sitting there. You were on the jaguar seat in the place of forgetting and remembering. You were sitting at a place of great power, a place where four conflicting energies meet and challenge each other. If you can place yourself between them and mediate their attractions, you will have great influence in your world. But as in all great things, there is great danger. If you falter and don't honor Crazy Woman, she might get a hold on you and destroy you."

"May I ask you a question?"

Zoila nodded.

"Are you saying that Rainbow Mother and Crazy Woman represent aspects of my own nature?"

"Of course. There are two kinds of female energy on the earth, not simply one. The earth is female, as I am sure Agnes has instructed you. A woman translates her energy in the form of the ecstatic Rainbow Mother or the nurturing Great Mother.

"You experienced the Great Mother, the nurturing mother, in the north," Zoila explained. "The great Chicomecoatl is known as the grandmother of the gods. She bore gifts of fruits and grains, was suckling the cornhusk baby, and her waist was encircled by seven snakes. Both of the great matriarchs are emissaries of very real hoops of energy. They each have their contrary and opposite pole. Crazy Woman is in the west across from the Rainbow Mother in the east. Opposite the Great Mother is the Death Mother or Coatlique, the snake goddess, in the south. She can be an instrument of your death. She carries poisonous reptiles in her arms and wears a robe of dead snakes. If you choose not to look at either of these noble matriarchs, Crazy Woman or the Death Mother, and honor their power, they can easily overpower you. Then you will be consumed by madness, depression, or even death."

"What must I do?"

"You must realize la Ultima Madre, realize who you are, and become who you are. Realize you belong to Rainbow Mother and embody her. The soul she has is the soul you have. For you, she is la Ultima Madre. You are the creative one who dances with dreams and visions. Haven't you always felt like you didn't belong?"

"I have always felt out of synch," I said.

"Yes, your way is very difficult, because your culture doesn't support its artists. Your culture accepts only the great nurturing matriarch, the type of woman who grows the corn and raises the children. These women love routine, get married, raise their children, and generally have a much easier time than their rainbow sisters. While the Rainbow Mothers are frustrated, unfulfilled, and perhaps alcoholics because of the expectations of others, the Great Mothers are the pillars of society. Until they reach midlife, that is. Then they find that their children are grown, and there is no one to nurture. At that point, their opposite energy, the Death Mother, comes close and tries to take them away."

"It sounds like a dangerous time," I said.

"Yes, when women understand their Ultima Madre, or final mother, they can build altars and fetishes of these powers. When they feel the influence of Crazy Woman or the Death Mother, in the form of depression or gloom, they can light candles and burn copal and honor her great power, the dark side. You see, her intent only defines your goodness and beauty. By honoring the dark side, you destroy her power over you. Then she can't take you."

"How do these teachings pertain to men?"

"This is a female earth. Men have these energies also, these hoops of power. They stand behind men and within women. They too must learn to honor the dark side. Where does the madman come from, but from Crazy Woman? It's the same."

I went to my room and sat on my bed for a long time, reflecting on this enormously important lesson. The images of the four sacred mothers seemed to hover above me. A cool current of wind blew through the open window and caressed me. I shivered.

Different passages of my life came to mind vividly. I saw images of a winter landscape with snow swirling in front of me. I was cross-country skiing with my husband, the winter before our divorce. If only I had known then what I had so recently learned about the two distinct differences in the translation of female energy. I realize now that neither of us had been right or wrong, even though we both appeared to be at fault to the other. We did not understand the other's needs. Of course we had so many confrontations, each blaming the other, that the marriage was eventually destroyed.

Without telling my husband, I had shopped for a special set of oil paints in tiny tubes that would fit in my pack along with rolled canvasses and a small waterproof tarp to sit on. When we stopped to rest, I spread out the tarp and laid the tubes of paint and brushes out to surprise him and for us both to use and enjoy.

"I'm starving," he said furiously. "I can't believe how selfish you are. I thought you packed the lunch."

I apologized. "But look," I said, gesturing toward the spectacular snow-blanketed landscape waiting to be captured by our paints.

He became even more enraged, livid. "Why didn't you bring food?" he yelled.

I tried to calm him and cajole him into a better humor. I explained that his spirit needed food too. But I soon realized that any attempt to pacify him by words alone would be futile. I gave him what little food I had thought to bring.

He was still angry days later. And this scenerio was repeated over and over again, typical of our marriage relationship. If I had understood that he was a nurturing type of man who, in turn, needs to be nurtured, I would have never brought up the suggestion of inspiration. He was not the sort who dreamed dreams or became excited over new ideas. Nor was he interested in aesthetics. He wanted a hefty beef sandwich so he could keep skiing. I could have happily starved while taking in the vastness and the beauty of the mountains.

I wanted to touch that sacred place in him, but I didn't know how. It is nearly impossible to reach a man—even a loving husband —whose intuitional side has closed off. Like so many men in today's society, my husband mistakenly believed sensitivity to be weakness. He was frightened of being healed because he couldn't identify his problem; nor could I. There was only emptiness and confusion for us both.

Agnes came through the door sipping on a green drink. "Agnes," I said, "I can see now that my marriage would never have worked. A nurturing husband and an ecstatic wife could never make it."

"Sometimes that makes for a very good marriage, if each appreciates the other's needs."

"I don't see how."

"It works very well for certain rainbow men or women," Agnes said. "Their lives are in chaos because they are always in the dream state. If they marry a nurturing type person, the nurturing partner is fulfilled by taking care of the rainbow partner. This is wonderful for both of them."

"But the nurturing person likes to know what you're doing all of the time, and that you're going to be home at five-thirty for dinner. For a rainbow person to be pinned down, well, I can't even think that way. In my marriage it lead to continuous fights and ruined the relationship."

"You're making the nurturing mother sound lesser in some way. But she is the great powerful mother of this earth. Without her, you would not have families. You wouldn't grow the corn. You would have absolute chaos."

"But Agnes, the rainbow person and the nurturing person would never communicate. And the rainbow person wants to communicate with the person that she loves more than anything in the world."

"If two rainbow people get together, they may forget to eat. They can starve to death, lost in their own chaos. To make a marriage work they have to become practical. If a rainbow person is deeply commited to work, and she finds a nurturing partner to look after her, then it's superior as long as the nurturing partner does not try to control and nail the rainbow partner's feet to the ground. Each has to see they are very different in their vision of the world, and then work with that."

The markings on a wooden wall
are howlings that a sun
can call
to be sleek pelicans
upon a beach
Our wings whistle
as we reach
the jaguar skies.

Michael McClure
"For Shirley and Wallace"

# Chapter 5
## Jaguar Woman

Agnes went down to dinner but told me to stay in the room. I was not to eat. The rain passed, and the full moon shone brilliantly, broken only by the tall branches of the cieba trees. Everything looked different. The nervous flutter of the birds subsided as darkness enfolded the ancient ruins of Uxmal.

Agnes and I sat on our red and black medicine blankets in the center of what Agnes told me was the Nunnery Quadrangle in the back of the Temple of the Magicians. A light, warm wind played with the silk fringes on our shawls. Our sacred medicine pipes lay between us as we sat facing each other. The mysterious stone and clay city around us loomed like a giant in the moonlight shadows. My doubts about why I was here had faded away with the smoke from our pipes. There was magic here, and I knew that great knowledge had been lost when the priests and priestesses of this city had been harmed. The magic of the earth beneath me rose up into my blood, and the earth took my spirit as her own. This certainly was a place where great wisdom was collected and shared.

Slowly, like phantoms in the night, other women joined us. I didn't know who they were, and not a word was spoken. We sat a long time, sharing the silence. Agnes told me to shut my eyes and clear my mind of thoughts, to concentrate on an inner flame. A clay flute sounded off to my left, and after a long time I opened my eyes. Several torches had been lit on the steps leading up to a low

building on the left of the quadrangle. A flat stone on four carved
stone legs reaching knee height was in its doorway. The women had
organized into two lines that fanned out down the stone stairs. A
woman stood before the raised stone. I could see copal smoke rising
from it, and all sorts of offerings and flowers had been placed there.
The smoke was so intense, it took me a moment to realize that the
woman had her back to us. She was wearing a jaguar skin robe. Her
arms and pawlike hands were outstretched in prayer, and then she
blew water onto the altar and smudged copal incense over her body,
purifying herself. She stood about twenty-five feet from us. She was
saying beautiful and melodic prayers rapidly in Mayan, and the
quadrangle resounded with her words. With the darkness the
ancient stone structure edged closer and loomed larger in my vision.
The warm night air settled in around us like a velvety cocoon,
shrouding us in a blanket of hypnotic pleasure.

The woman at the altar slowly turned. I gasped, and Agnes briefly
rested her hand on my knee to still me. Great billows of gray-white
smoke shone around the woman and snaked through the night. A
ghostly figure, she was wearing a white jaguar mask that looked like
it was carved out of stone. The black spots of the jaguar skin
accented the shadows. With outstretched arms, she called my name.

I gathered my pipe and offering bundle and walked up the stairs
to her. Agnes followed me. I walked through the cloud of copal
smoke and sat across from the woman, who had seated herself on
the other side of the altar. I sat on a grass mat and Agnes sat to my
left, also holding her pipe. Then Agnes handed the woman her pipe
across the altar and she laid it there. I repeated the gesture with my
pipe. My eyes were riveted on this woman. She held her power with
such catlike majesty that I was transfixed and terrified at the same
time. I knew she was a woman, but at certain moments during her
ceremony, when she squared her shoulders or gripped something
with her strong hands or put on the jaguar gloves, I could have
sworn she was a man. She looked at me steadily. In broken English,
slightly muffled by the mask, she said, "You have shown me that
you can serve the shaman sisters. Now I know that you can serve
the Spirit."

Deftly she removed the mask, turning it over. She poured a liquid into it and drank from it briefly. Her face was painted solid black, and I could see only her eyes, which shone like the moon. She handed the mask to me. I took it, holding her eyes with mine. The mask felt smooth and heavy, like a rock. I sipped something that tasted like wine and then placed the mask back into her painted hands. She replaced it over her face. Although I could not see her clearly, and never did, I knew she was familiar. I offered her the bundle I had brought. Agnes had instructed me to bring liquor, white copal, tobacco, chocolate, incense, candles, and many flowers. She accepted it with many beautiful Mayan words and laid the contents out on the altar. From her mouth she sprayed some of the liquor onto the altar near several objects standing nearest me, behind lighted candles.

I looked at the beautiful array of sacred objects on the altar. There were blossoms everywhere, candles, stones, sticks with feathers, hollowed-out stones with objects in them, a wrapped bundle, a crucifix, herbs, and many more objects obscured by the shadows. I felt an intangible force field running from the altar to me, coursing like a finite magnetism through the trunk of my body.

"Knowledge is recognition," she said, watching my eyes caress her altar. "You recognize her, don't you? Now you know of her power, even though you don't understand it."

Sitting across from me curled up on her mat like a large feline, she nodded. She began speaking in a forceful way that took me immediately into the most sacred spot inside of myself, my medicine place.

"Stand," she said. She adjusted me until I was facing outward and could see the two lines of women still standing on the stone steps. They seemed to be watching attentively. "For too long," the priestess said, "our sisters have lived without taking their power. You have a great enemy, the one with red hair who is near you now. You stalked him once, but that was long ago. Out of your feelings of fear and guilt, you have become his prey. He has injured the lights around you. He stalks you now. The stalker must be stalked. We

here are your sisters. What happens to you happens to us. Hold
forth your hands."

I held them out to her. She took off her pawlike gloves and
placed them on my hands. I moved my fingers, and sharp claws
sprang out. For a moment my vision blurred but then became
extremely acute. Jaguar Woman drew off her robe and fastened it
around my shoulders. The women on the steps came silently forward
and encircled me in a half-moon. The women were all staring at me
and seemed to be focusing their attention on my navel. Behind me I
felt Jaguar Woman with her arms upraised. I felt her power and the
power of the altar radiating toward me. I looked at Agnes for
reassurance, but she had the same intent look as the other women. I
was getting warm, feverish.

All at once I shot upward out of my body and was flying over the
tops of trees. Then I was on the ground, running amazingly fast
through the jungle, which I seemed to understand remarkably well. I
halted and sniffed, then turned on a diagonal southward. In that
instant I realized I was a jaguar spirit, and the scent I was following
belonged to Red Dog.

I bounded up a hill over tightly curled grasses and then slowed to
a stealthy, noiseless gait. From behind a tree I saw Red Dog with
his back to me. I crouched, ready to spring. He turned and saw me,
a look of terror in his eyes. I growled and he stamped his foot and
shouted. "Eeeeiii! Eeeeiii!" he yelled. He started spinning until he
completely disappeared into a funnel of wind that moved off quickly.
I charged at this whirlwind but it kept just ahead of me. I wanted
to leap into it and claw it to pieces. As I pursued my prey, I felt my
body breaking up.

I woke up in my bed at the hacienda to find Agnes rubbing ice
over my forehead and cheeks.

If you wander far enough
you will come to it
and when you get there
they will give you a place to sit
for yourself only, in a nice chair,
and all your friends will be there
with smiles on their faces
and they will likewise all have places.

Robert Creeley
"Oh No"

# Chapter 6
# The Green Dwarf

A great rumbling in the distance jerked us out of my story and a stillness came over the cabin. A sudden gusty draft blew the lantern out, and we sat looking around in the firelight. We had all been so engrossed in the jaguar chase in the Yucatán that we had to blink to remember where we were. A wolf began to sing in the distance. Then another wolf answered off to the right. Behind us, several other wolves answered. Ordinarily I loved to hear them, but tonight in the strange stillness they made the hackles rise on my neck.

"Going to snow," Ruby said, lighting her pipe.

"Hope we don't get snowbound," Agnes said.

"What do you mean?" I asked nervously.

"Hear the silence. Listen and feel how much warmer it is. It means snow's coming and a heavy snow can be up to the top of the cabin." Agnes got up and relit the lantern.

That night as the snow fell, I dreamed of the beautiful man in the butterfly tree. He stood there near me, as he had when I had first seen him. There was a gentleness about him that was irresistible. I wanted to go with him, to lose myself in his arms. Another life floated in the distance, where there was no purpose, no destiny, just a sensual enjoyment of the earth and her fruits. A cathedral stood in the background. It was night, and the beautiful man and I wanted to go inside. But the doors were locked. Butterflies landed all over us, and we lay on the ground in soft

enjoyment. It was true—I wanted to stay with him and never return
to life as I knew it.

I awoke not wanting to talk much, still thinking about my dream
of the young hero in the butterfly tree. When I finally did speak,
my voice was a horrid croak. My throat was swollen and irritated,
and my words caught in midsyllable to add to the rasp.

Agnes seemed unusually concerned. "These things can become
serious if you don't take care of them," she said, peering into my
mouth. She took me to one side and sat me down.

"Okay, Mom," I said, feeling completely in her power.

She returned with a bundle she had taken from a drawer and
opened it on the table. July and Ruby were asked to stand about six
paces behind me and to hold their attention on the small of my
back. Agnes took a skillet containing smoking cedar chips from the
stove and circled me four times. She set the skillet on a rock at the
foot of my chair. Using a spotted eagle feather, she fanned the
smoke over my body, then smudged it onto my face.

"Close your eyes," she ordered. "Use your imagination."

She began to talk in a soft voice of places we had been. I saw
images of peaceful mountains, flowery meadows, and beautiful
familiar places that we had shared and loved together. I went into a
deeply relaxed state.

"Now," she said, "I am going to blow some smoke in your face.
It is a powerful hallucinogenic smoke. Keep your eyes closed, and
don't fight it."

I heard Ruby say to July, "That's too strong for Lynn."

"I said don't fight it," Agnes commanded in a most authoritative
voice.

"I won't," I squeaked.

I felt Agnes's breath on my face, smelled sweet smoke, and
inhaled it.

"Breathe deep," she said.

I did, coughed, then continued to breathe in the smoke.

After several minutes she spoke. "That's enough. Now imagine
your consciousness has taken the form of a little green man. Assume
for a while that this little green man represents the most sacred part

of yourself and is one of the highest spirits of our tradition. He is
the guardian spirit of medicine people. He appears to be a dwarf
and he carries a bow and many sacred arrows. He casts a great light
around him that enables him to see in dark places. Do you see
him?"

"Yes," I said softly.

"Describe him to me."

I did see him perfectly. In fact, nothing else existed. "He is very
small," I said. "About two feet tall but powerfully built. He is
completely clothed in green as if his skin, face, everything were dyed
that color. He wears a green eagle feather and has a quiver of
several arrows. He is waiting. I sense that he is extremely clever. His
emerald green eyes are shining brightly. I believe him to have
mighty powers, and I think he is a direct messenger from the Great
Spirit."

"Good," Agnes said. "I want you to see him taking a journey
through the interior of your body. Take a deep breath of the cedar
smoke, and relax yourself completely. Now see the little green man
entering with his illumination into the top of your head. He is your
consciousness, so follow along with him. Can you see the inside of
your head?"

After several minutes I could.

I answered her, "Yes."

Agnes's words had worked like a magic spell. What I was
experiencing was incredible. All around me was my brain cavity,
pulsating, pink, and healthy.

Agnes asked, "Do you see anything unusual?"

"Yes. Behind my eyes I see a large, perfect crystal with a pyramid
inside of it."

"Be more explicit. Where exactly is it located?"

"It sits behind what I call my third eye and what you call my
medicine eye. I assume it is the crystal placed inside me by Butterfly
Woman."

The green dwarf materialized in front of me again, and I gasped.
Gently, Agnes asked me to continue.

"The dwarf is picking up the crystal and examining it. It has an

extremely beautiful light, prisms of color, visions, people from my
past, and people I don't recognize. It's all moving in and out of
focus. Now the dwarf is taking some of the light and visions and
people and putting them into his pocket. They don't belong to him.
They're mine." I began to cry, not understanding why the dwarf
would do this.

"Ask him why he is taking some of your light and why he is
taking some of your visions and people."

I asked him as I became a form within my own form. The dwarf
looked into my spirit eyes and said, "When you learn to see properly
through this crystal, then I will return this light and these visions
and people. For now they are too much for you. They could burn
you up. You are not yet ready." He patted his pocket full of glowing
light. "They will be safe with me."

"Ask him to teach you how to use the crystal," Agnes said.

I did. He gently placed his green fingers on my spirit eyes. Then
he took one of his arrows out of his quiver and said, "I must shoot
this arrow through your forehead to make way for the light.
Sometimes I shoot arrows of illumination and sometimes I shoot
arrows into people who say bad things. For you, an arrow of
illumination. Are you ready?"

"Yes, I think so."

"Give me a thought," he said.

I sent him a thought of lightning.

"Give me a word," he said.

"Lightning."

"Thoughts and words are like lightning in a storm. Lightning is a
gift from the mountain spirits and, like words and thoughts,
announces its presence and protection to a new shaman. It is an
electrical shock." Just as he said the last word he shot the arrow. It
went through my forehead like a lightning bolt. When the arrow
struck it glittered brightly. It did not hurt, but it certainly jarred me.
He picked up the crystal and held it up. It gleamed and sent off
rays of light like compressed rainbows.

"Now look carefully and *see* me," the dwarf said.

I felt a subtle shift in the way I perceived things. He pushed the

crystal nearer, so that I gazed deeply into it. I saw my own
reflection; I had bangs and a short haircut. Then for a moment I
saw Butterfly Woman. Suddenly there was an explosion of light, and
I saw the green dwarf was a shell. He was empty, and only a great
light animated him. It scared me, because I realized then that we
are all empty shells. We are nothing.

"There," he said, smiling. "Now you see we are nothing and
everything. Ho!" He did a little dance that made me laugh. His
arms and legs shuffled back and forth. He halted. "That's how you
do it." His emerald eyes twinkled. "I believe you may be ready for
one of these visions I've got here. What do you think?"

I nodded my head.

Very slowly he pulled a corner of light covered with images of
stark cliffs and an ancient pueblo out of his pocket. I realized the
images were from sometime in the future. I was with someone, but
I could see only his back. I knew that I loved this person deeply,
and that through him a great deal had been revealed to me. The
feeling was completely ecstatic, and tears started to well up in my
eyes.

"Oops, too soon." The dwarf dropped the light back into his
pocket and out of sight.

"But wait! I want to see, please."

"Nope, out of the question," he said briskly. "We better move
on."

I heard Agnes speak, and it was as though she were a great
distance from me.

"Now move with the dwarf down into your throat, Lynn," she
suggested.

It didn't take much encouragement. I followed him down into my
throat, wanting very much to become a pickpocket and get the
vision back. But I didn't dare.

"What do you see?" Agnes asked.

"I'm looking," I said. "There's a red and pink light here, and
everything just looks pretty much like a throat."

"Is there anything unusual?"

"Not really."

"Take your spirit hands and touch the walls of your throat, and tell me how it feels."

"Actually, it feels dry and too hard."

"Press against the walls harder."

"They resist me."

"Where is the dwarf?"

"He's sitting over by the wall on something."

"What is he sitting on?"

"It looks like a piece of obsidian."

"Go closer, and look at it carefully."

"Oh! Now I see. It's not obsidian. He's sitting on a big crow."

"Ask him why he's sitting on the crow."

I asked him and he said, "So that you would be sure to see the crow."

"I do see him," I said. "Why don't you stand up so I can see him even better."

The dwarf stood up, shrugging his shoulders. "If you like."

The crow strutted around and fluffed his feathers.

"Ask the crow what he's doing in your throat," Agnes said.

When I did, he answered me in a croak not unlike the croak of my own voice earlier that morning. "I am keeper of the earthly laws. You usually express them well. But you are finding it difficult to talk about all the many things you have been learning."

"What can I do?" I asked him as he was flapping his blue-black wings.

"You can let me out of your throat."

"Oh, I'd be happy to."

Agnes prompted me. "Ask him what else you can do."

I did, and the crow pecked at the lining of my throat and said, "You need to remember the importance of saying what you need to say. If you hold your power in your throat, I will have to return and I can cause your throat to hurt very much." To emphasize his point, he pecked me again. It produced a painful sensation. The crow cocked his head and fixed me with a gleaming eye.

Agnes asked, "What does the dwarf think of all this?"

I asked him, and he said, "I think you must make a throat bundle for your altar."

"I don't know what a throat bundle is," I said.

The dwarf scratched his green head and put his right foot forward. "Take the visions that you have had of me and the crow and your throat. Make an image of these feelings and things you have experienced."

"An image?"

"Yes."

"What do you mean by an image of these things?"

"Your throat feels dry and constricted, doesn't it?"

"It certainly does."

"Then wrap something tight so that it gives the impression of the discomfort in your throat. Pray with it. Put power into it. Place a crow feather, something green, a crystal, and something that represents light and all that you have witnessed in the bundle. Do a ceremony, and you will have a bundle that has power. It is a gift, a blessing, from the Great Spirit. He sends this knowledge, these arrows, so that you may live."

"Should I let the crow out now?"

"Of course. Take my hand, and let the crow perch on your left hand. Now follow me out through the top of your head." I felt a sensation of being drawn upward by a magnetic force. The green man was at my side, and it was like riding up in a cosmic elevator. "That's right," he shouted. "Now fly out into the universe toward the Pleiades. Do you see them?"

"Yes, I do." I was hurtling upward at an incredible velocity. I saw the sun as just another star among the infinite galaxies.

"Now let the crow go into the light of the seven sisters," the green dwarf said.

"Go," I said. The crow sprang from my hand and flew into the Pleiades. I turned to look at the green dwarf, but he had vanished.

"They're gone," I said.

"Yes. How does your throat feel?" Agnes asked.

I cleared my throat and swallowed. I was completely cured. "Wonderful!"

Agnes put her hand on my forehead. "Take several deep breaths, and feel your life force coming back into your body. Feel the power of Mother Earth in the soles of your feet. Feel her energies coming back into your legs like a warm wave of water at the ocean shore."

My throat felt fine, but my body was wooden. Slowly, as Agnes pulled the life energy back into me, the stiffness went away. She tapped me on the forehead. I opened my eyes and wiggled my toes. I felt great, but also, like I had been on a trip around the universe and back.

"Better now?" Agnes asked.

"Much."

"Good." She sat in a chair and began beading a moccasin.

I swallowed several times, and my throat felt perfectly normal. "That was magic, Agnes. I feel great. What was the powerful hallucinogen you used? I don't think I've ever had an experience as vivid as that."

Agnes chuckled and turned her face up from the beadwork. "That powerful hallucinogen was ordinary pipe tobacco."

Ruby and July laughed like a couple of clowns.

"Lynn can't help it if she's suggestible," Agnes offered by way of encouragement. I felt slightly foolish. "It is good medicine that the green dwarf came to her so quickly. These things are real, Lynn."

"Who was that rascal?" I asked.

"The green dwarf is very sacred, and he carries the sacred arrows of the people."

"But what was he doing in my head?"

"You were getting sick. You held too much light. The dwarf knew this, and so what better place to help you with your vision eye."

"Will I ever see him again?"

"That depends on you, doesn't it?"

"Yes, I guess so." I paused to think for a moment. "Was that my imagination?"

"Do you feel better?"

"Completely."

"Well then, what does it matter? Why pick at a bone when it has no meat on it? In other words, your question is irrelevant. What is relevant is that you were getting sick—sicker than you know. Now you're well, and that's what's important."

"Can you talk to me about the throat bundle?"

Ruby came over and set two cups of tea on the table for me and Agnes. She shook her head back and forth. "Talk, talk, talk. Sometimes I think Lynn is just talk, talk, talk. Talking so much gets on my nerves."

"I'd be happy to talk to you about throat bundles, Lynn," Agnes said, ignoring Ruby.

"Humph," Ruby said. "Some thanks I get for being so concerned." She started ordering July around, making her straighten up the cabin.

Agnes smiled and continued, "A throat bundle is like any other bundle. It is part of your personal government. When archeologists uncover artifacts and sacred bundles, they say all kinds of stupid things. Sacred bundles are sacred; to gut them is against our beliefs. Let them make their own sacred bundles, and quit fooling around looting someone else's."

"That's the first time I've heard either of you say anything worth saying since we got back," Ruby said in an agitated voice. She stood near July, giving her instructions on how to sweep the floor properly. "Don't throw away the bark. We can use that as kindling. Where's your brain?"

Poor July.

Agnes completely ignored both of them. "Lynn, pay attention to me if you wish to learn of throat bundles."

I apologized, and she went on. "What you put in your throat bundle is self-understanding from your own personal visions, and it is a part of your truth, no other. In making a personal bundle you take something intangible—a feeling, a dream, even a problem—from inside yourself, and you manifest it into the physical world so that you can examine it and use it. This process of transformation from spirit into substance enables you to heal others, because through your action of making it, you heal yourself. The green dwarf has given you a great insight into the way you hold your power in your throat. Like many people, women in particular, we are told to hold our tongue."

"Good idea," Ruby said.

Agnes stared at the floor smiling and then looked back at me.
"Children are told to speak when spoken to. We as women are
taught that to speak of our power is to be shunned by most of
society. When you listen to the voices of many men and women,
you hear a strangled sound. And it's no wonder. Women's voices are
often weak or a monotone or barely audible. Voices need to be open
and free, so that energy can flow through the throat center. We
hold our enlightenment there. If energy is trapped in the throat, it
can't move up into the crown of the head. That's why we get sore
throats, thyroid problems, or diseases such as throat cancer.
Whenever you have an energy knot like that, it will eventually cause
disease."

"Is it the same in the rest of the body?"

"Yes, of course. By now you must recognize that this is why a
medicine person begins working with his or her apprentice's body.
Think of your body as a road map. When seen this way, it speaks of
your spiritual, emotional, and psychic development. When I look at
you, I can see where your holes are. As you know, I see where you
hold your energy and where you leak it out. When a person holds
energy in the heart I know that that person has trauma there, is
afraid to open up and love, and could develop any number of heart
problems. You, however, if anything, are too open and trusting."

"Why do you say that?"

"It's obvious. You care too much, and people can hurt you too
easily. That is why we are trying to toughen you up, see?"

"All right, is my throat OK now?"

"You tell me what is true."

"It feels normal."

"Then it is, and you've taken care of the problem. We are the
only ones who can heal ourselves—sometimes with assistance,
sometimes not. Trust yourself. Listen to your own voice. It's deep
and open. Sing a song for me."

I sang the lyrics to a popular song. Indeed, my voice was better
than ever. I got up and saw that July and Agnes were staring at me.
They resumed work immediately.

"Now what are you going to do?" Agnes asked.

"I'll make my bundle," I said.

July was mopping. Ruby had the whole countertop filled with dishes and boxes of meat. The cabin was suddenly unbearably tiny. I wondered how I could ever find the necessary items to make my throat bundle. It seemed impossible.

Agnes said, as if she had followed my thoughts, "You can do it. Everything you need is here. The things you need are always there; you need to be smart enough to find them." She went back to her beading. It was as if I had been dismissed from her consciousness.

I scratched around for a while and then went to the irregular window. Looking out the glass pane at the green-and-yellow flickerings of the northern lights, I felt displaced. I was somewhere that time had forgotten, in a wintry fairy tale. I touched the cold glass window panel, and my finger left a dot, an insignificant spot in the scheme of things, a fleeting dot that closed in on itself and obscured the Christmas tree lights that played there. I have only a moment, I thought, to figure this all out. I closed my eyes for a second and saw the green dwarf. He was staring at me curiously.

I turned quickly and wandered quietly around the cabin, picking up pieces of leather, because that's how my throat had felt, a small crystal that reflected the lights, a tiny bird skeleton, a crow feather, and a piece of shiny green metal. Sure enough, all that I needed was there, just as Agnes had told me. I was delighted, and for the next several hours I burned cedar and sage and sweet grass from my pipe bag. I sang power songs softly to the birth of my new throat bundle.

I awoke the next morning to the smell of oatmeal cooking. After eating, Agnes stood me up and looked at me carefully. She told me that there was a tenseness around my eyes and jaw. She handed me a shovel and had me dig out snow from the doorway and around the sheds until dark. Afterward, we all gathered again around the stove. July and Agnes were beading, and Ruby was fixing leather goods.

I resumed the story of my travels in the Yucatán.

Before I enter the rooms of your solitude
in my living form, trailing my shadow,

I shall have come unseen. Upstairs and down with you
and out across road and rocks to the river

to drink the cold spray. You will believe
a bird flew by the window, a wandering bee
buzzed in the hallway, a wind
rippled the bronze grasses. Or will you

know who it is?

Denise Levertov
"The Presence"

# Chapter 9
# A Balance of Power

I slept that night in a hammock in Zoila's hut. The next day I helped her in the garden. We played with the children and two new puppies. She showed me how to make a proper tortilla. After dinner, when the village was quiet and the children asleep, she took me out to a flat stone. Leaning her back against a cieba tree, she laid out some of her altar bundles and unwrapped them. She sang songs and burned incense as she worked.

"I have dreamed you. Would you like to know what I see?" she asked me. She seemed to be in a heightened state of tension.

"Yes," I replied.

"You have a lot to learn, but I think you are sincere with your books. You are giving people another place to go." She paused. "When I say a lot to learn, I mean that you are able to learn it. Your road will let you. You are strong enough to do the thing you feel is right, and you are still very young in your love for femaleness. And I don't mean feminine. The discovery of the firstness of the mother is every shaman's well-guarded personal vision. You want everyone to know, and to that I say good luck." She paused a moment. The candlelight flickered across her face, making her eyelids seem to open and then half close in thought.

"Stand," she said. "You have enemies. Three of them are draggers. They will sidetrack your energies. They resent you and are jealous." She lifted my arms and took a pot of smoking copal and smudged it under my armpits. "Where the sun doesn't look, that's where they try to enter."

We sat down again.

"Your altar is pulling me," I said, rubbing my heart.

"We do not call this an altar, although that is what it is in your way. We call her the mask or the face of the earth. She attracts you because she is of my dreams and my visions, and you feel my friendship with her."

We sat for several moments, and then I asked, "Are my enemies serious trouble?"

"Remember that I am divining the probable, not the future. Your three enemies are not serious. But there is a man who sings your song in the way that a lover sings for his intended wife. He is on your trail. I see a dead coyote. He has tried to send a dark female spirit. Very dark. She has short black hair, like a man's, and tries to make friends with your spirits. She's like a dead person—not attached to you, but she's chasing you."

"What do you mean like a dead person?" Hackles of fear were edging up my spine.

"She is not alive in the physical world, but she wasn't buried properly, so she needs a body that she likes. If she finds that, she may kill that person and then go on to the next body."

"Wasn't buried properly?" Now I was scared.

"She has to be buried properly," Zoila said.

"How do I bury her?"

"I don't mean physically dig a hole. You have to pay her debts, and in that way she can be accepted into the other world. She hasn't been accepted, because she was not buried well. If you can pay her debts, then you can get her power. That's big medicine. Then she goes on to the other side. You have to discover what she needs."

"But how do I do that?"

Zoila handed me a small pouch from which dangled a leather thong with beads at the end. "Here. Put a little bit of what's in here in a cup of water before you sleep. Burn some copal. Follow your dreams. You will know. She will make you learn how to fight."

I knew that the man on my trail was Red Dog. I had thought coming down to the Yucatán would have thrown him off my scent completely. After the Jaguar ceremony I knew I was wrong.

"Don't worry, my daughter," Zoila said. "You are here now, and I am pleased."

"Thank you for dreaming me . . ."

"You will learn the face of the earth soon."

After many prayers, she wrapped the objects on the stone altar into many bundles, and the ceremony was over. I left and went back to the hacienda to be with Agnes.

I walked into the room and sat down on the bed. I took out the pouch Zoila had given me and emptied some of the contents into my hand. "What do you suppose this is?" I asked Agnes.

Agnes came over and held my outstretched palm in both of hers. She smelled the tiny particles of bark and pieces of white leaves carefully. "Smells like herbs to me," she said, pursing her lips and raising her eyebrows.

"Agnes, I know that. But what herbs? Are they going to make me crazy?"

"Make you crazy? Ha! That's an impossibility." Agnes looked at me as if I were already nuts and then laughed.

I stared at her for a long time and then blurted out, "Do you think Red Dog knows where we are?"

"It's probable." She was still smiling.

"Why are you laughing? This is not funny!"

"Red Dog isn't funny, but you are."

"If Red Dog is around, then he knows about our ceremonies."

"He doesn't know about the ceremonies. But he knows something is going on."

"Is he really here in the Yucatán?" I placed a pillow over my stomach and returned the herbs to the pouch.

"I sense that he is. You saw him in your Jaguar dream, didn't you?"

"Yes, I think I did. I don't want to die in the Yucatán," I said.

Agnes reached over and took the pouch from me. She rolled it back and forth over her palm, seeming to be lost in thought. I

watched her lined and wrinkled face, and it seemed to smooth out
younger for several moments. Then she turned away. Finally she
said, "This is serious. Red Dog needs you now. He thinks he's on
the trail of something big, and he knows you can lead him to it.
The spirit that Zoila saw, she's out there, but she's of no danger yet
and may never be. She's waiting for him to send her. He could
change his mind. She's stalking. Be aware of that like you are of
your own death. In that way she can become a great ally. Just like
you, she wants to live. She can live off you, or she can be sent
where she belongs. I want that to be your choice. You are no
victim."

"How do I send her where she belongs?"

"If you choose to take her power, you can. You can take her on,
and learn to bury her. But to bury her, you must learn to fight. To
take her on is to make an agreement to fight your own dark side.
'Bury her' is Zoila's way of saying you must war with the devouring
woman within yourself. In this instance, another word for 'war' is
'balance.' To balance your dark side with your beauty brings you to
power. But remember, it's your own reflection that you're fighting."

"Have I not learned to fight?" I thought of Manitoba, the scene
of a conflict between Red Dog and myself; I had stolen back a
marriage basket from him so I could return it to the Dreamers, the
sacred circle of women elders.

"In some ways."

"What do I need to know?"

"That is for your dreams. Zoila is right. You must learn to follow
them. It is not for me to tell you."

"Should I take this tonight?" I indicated the pouch.

"No," she said, handing it back to me. "Hold all that we have
spoken of, understand it. You will feel her stalking you, or she may
go away. You will know when it is time to dream her. Then take
the herbs."

"Thank you, Agnes."

I placed the pouch in my bundle and turned out the lights. I
crawled into my bed and looked into the darkness for several
minutes. "Are all of these women part of the sisterhood of the

shields, Agnes? Sometimes I feel like the sisterhood doesn't really
exist."

"Why is that?"

"Because whenever we meet, it's like a dream. Everything
becomes so powerful and extraordinary. Then I'm so knocked out
that I sleep for a day. When I wake up I've had remarkable dreams,
and I don't know what is real and what is illusion."

"Is that so?" Agnes chuckled.

"Yes. For instance, who owns this hacienda?"

"The sisterhood is not a club, Lynn. The sisterhood exists only in
terms of self-realization. We don't have scheduled meetings, but we
meet. It's not a sorority or a bridge party. We don't elect
representatives. We assume power. You are here, and that should be
sufficient for you to understand its validity. Sometimes a sister falls
from the path and is left with only glimpses of what she
experienced. She doubts the sisterhood and goes so far as to say she
was self-deceived. When you hear a sister discussing her place and
prestige within us, you will know that she is dancing on the rim of
forgetfulness. She is going off on her long sleep and will probably
never return."

"Any woman can belong to the sisterhood, Lynn. Many spend
their lifetime in search of us and never find anything but their own
meandering trail. Others come into our midst without the slightest
effort. If a woman were to ask me if I were a member of the
sisterhood, I could answer in all honesty, 'no.' Because what I would
mean by the sisterhood and what she would mean by the sisterhood
would be two entirely different things. Go to sleep now."

"Good night, Agnes."

That night I dreamed I was standing on a lava cliff overlooking
the ocean. The moon shone like pieces of silver mica on the water.
The waves rolled in with long, heavy swells, breaking over the rocks
in great sprays of white foam. Ruby Plenty Chiefs stood with me
holding my hand. We dove off the cliff into the surf. She still held
my hand as we swam down deep into the sea. We could breathe
and were comfortable as we turned beneath the waves. We were as
night passing through an underworld of primordial fish. I heard a

creation chant being uttered: "It is the god who enters, not as a human does he enter." I was following Ruby, swimming in slow, undulating movements, as we were both turning into one great sea serpent. We became a serpent and caused the waters to recede. I felt the union of the earth and the skies, and we as women spirits united with the earth substance and the first people were born.

I awoke early the next morning, feeling like I was still floating in the womb of the sea, feeling like Ruby had held me all night long with the comforting arms of a mother. I thought about blind Ruby for a long time that morning. She had been a medicine woman for me and had taught me about the ancient knowledge of shield making. Her people call her the keeper of the Face. She had dreamed me last night and given me a medicine dream. She had taught me something about the balance between male and female. When I told Agnes about it I had to laugh, because Ruby had truly comforted my fear away in the dream. Usually she terrified me beyond speech. I thought of the first time I had ever seen her. She had stood on the wooden porch of her cabin, brandishing a butcher knife, her blind eyes angry and shining like the blue eyes of a malamute at bay, and ordered me to help her skin out two deer that lay at her feet. Perhaps she would join us in the Yucatán.

We seek not rest but transformation.
We are dancing through each other as doorways.
We are ripples crossing and fusing, journeying and returning
from the core of the apple, the eye of the mandala,
the cave in the heart of the rose,
the circle without boundaries centered on silence.

Marge Piercy
"Circling"

# Chapter 8
# La Caldera and the Sacred Spiral

After dinner Agnes went back to the hacienda and I lay back in a hammock under the thatched overhang and listened to the sound of the wind and the chattering noises of the night. Soon I was fast asleep. Zoila's throaty song to the eastern sky woke me at dawn. I felt sluggish and incapable of exerting myself. New light from the rising sun splashed over us and made my eyes blink. For a moment I felt as though I were living in another lifetime.

I took a deep breath of warm fresh air. The scent of cooking tortillas contrasted with the fecund garden soil. The hammock swayed gently, and I started to doze off again. I was soon floating on a warm sweet wave of oblivion when, with no warning, my hammock took a dramatic swing. I came to my senses at once, barely landing on my feet. "Zoila, you scared me."

"You frighten easily." She had a wide smile, showing two rows of beautiful white teeth. I felt the power of her eyes, which were not smiling. "It is time to track the sun, my lazy, indolent daughter. We have a long trail to bridge today. Be alert and intelligent. Salute the sun, the Great Chief, as your teacher Agnes calls this essential star. Hold up your arms to Venus. She precedes the sun and is called the Sweeper of the Path."

I did as I was told. First I prayed to the eastern horizon, where the sun was a liquid silver oval set in the hazy purple sky. Then I prayed to Venus, the morning star still shining in the heavens. As I stood there I was taken by the beauty in front of me.

Zoila interrupted my sublime feelings. "Go eat," she said.

"Have you eaten, Zoila?" I asked. Zoila's demeanor was decidedly different from the night before.

"Yes, before sunrise. Take some fruit from the trees. There are tortillas inside."

I picked an avocado and a mango and went inside the house. It was silent; no familiar sounds of family life. An old yellow dog slept on the doorstep. I tripped over a corner of an Indian rug on the hard-packed dirt floor. Then I burned my finger on the frying pan while removing a tortilla. "Ouch!" I yowled, licking my finger and blowing on it.

Zoila laughed. "You've really got it in for yourself, don't you?" She tapped on the floor with her bamboo walking stick and continued laughing.

I asked if I could examine the staff she held in her left hand.

"Yes," she said. She handed it to me. "It is the mark of the *chiman*, or shamaness."

Tracing my index finger down the many long grooves, I asked, "What do these lines mean?"

"It is not as simple as it looks. The top lines represent the seven heavenly layers, or facets. The bottom lines represent the five layers of the lower world. In the old way, the creator deity lives in the seventh heaven and carries the sun. The sun is not a deity. The death god dwells in the fifth level of the underworld."

I handed the cane back to Zoila and remarked on the craftsmanship involved in carving the symbols.

"I carved it," she said. "Hurry and eat. We will speak more of this walking stick later. Now we must go with the sun to la caldera in the west."

"Doesn't that mean 'cauldron'?"

"Yes, this is the cauldron of the earth mother."

I ate my tortillas and, fruit in hand, followed Zoila out the door. She headed due west. Her brisk stride reminded me of the way Agnes walked. I have always liked to walk slowly, so it was a big effort to keep up with her pace. We followed a trail through low jungle and dense undergrowth. It was rough going.

Zoila used her staff like a third leg, moving it in unison with her right leg as she walked. She wore a thin white *huipile* and a blue woven skirt. She did not speak nor did she look back at me. Occasionally the trail would become completely overgrown, and I would see the flash of Zoila's machete. The sun was getting high in the sky when we began to climb. The Yucatán seems so flat and the foliage so dense, that I easily lost perspective on elevations. I heard the far-off sound of rushing water. The trees became taller, and soon we were in a high jungle with screeching green and yellow birds and a clamor of insects. The trees were covered with air plants bearing colorful blooming stalks. Long flowering vines hung from high trees. Through the swaying branches I could see low magenta-colored hills in the distance. They gave me the impression of having just been born from the jungle floor. I was getting tired. Still I heard the surging of water.

Zoila stopped and pointed to a ledge in front of us. We had climbed to a considerable height. Pointing with her walking stick, she said, "Here is where we meet the guardian of la caldera. We are on the east lip of la caldera. It is called the Place of Acknowledging, or the Place of the First Ceremony. Now we are going to have a ceremony to introduce you to Tlazolteatl, the goddess of the shamaness and magicians. She will show you the sacred spiral and many aspects of yourself. Come here. I will conduct you over the trail."

I followed Zoila as she walked over to a flat place. She pointed downward with her staff. I gasped. The jungle below us formed an enormous crater, and we were standing on the rim. The canyon was so deep that I couldn't see the bottom; it was obscured in mist. To my right was a jagged trail, a tiny ledge carved into the rock. I followed it with my eyes as it curved out of sight. The narrow path spiraled around and around inside of la caldera, down to the center. I laughed, but my stomach turned over.

Wide-eyed, I grabbed Zoila's arm. "Zoila, there's no way that I can go down that trail. I'm not good at heights. I'm not sure that I could ever make it." Tears were beginning to come.

"Let's get started." Zoila promptly scurried off and left me. I was dismayed. I would never venture one foot on that treacherous precipice. I stayed put.

"Damn it, Zoila," I wailed. "Don't leave me here. Can't you see I'm terrified? I can't do this. I just can't."

"Agnes said that you had courage. Perhaps you don't. Now you'll never see what's at the bottom."

I didn't have much choice. Zoila was about to disappear out of sight. I had come here to learn something from her, and, like it or not, I had to trust her.

"Wait a minute," I called.

I put one sandaled foot in front of the other, pressed against the ledge, and started. I knew I had to get control of my thoughts, or even better, not think at all. If I thought about it, I would be frozen with terror. I started after Zoila. Pieces of rock crumbled under my sandals, and rolled off the ledge, bouncing down out of sight. I tried not to look down. Tears were stinging my eyes. I was fearful, and knew I was not a skilled enough climber to navigate this narrow path. I was sure that I would momentarily slip and fall to my death.

The trail became even narrower, barely the breadth of my foot. I gasped for air, remembering to breathe and trying to relax. I didn't dare stop, and forced my will to pull my body ahead. I rounded the edged of the cliff. Zoila was in view, walking slowly and carefully, like a mountain goat. She moved more quickly when the trail permitted.

Because of my fear of heights, my mind didn't want my body to continue. But some deep longing made me willing to follow Zoila. It was as if all my concepts of self had exploded in my head, leaving me with only my will power to help me survive. My mind and its fear were useless on this precarious pathway. I was battling with my conception of who I was and what I could do. Knowing I couldn't do it, I did it anyway. This process produced a numbness of thought, so my fear did not paralyze me. As we slowly traversed around and down, I became more sure of myself, letting go of my first level of terror. As we went farther, other, deeper levels of terror became released, until an ecstatic feeling flooded through my being.

Just as I had gained some confidence, we came to a sheer cliff where the trail had crumbled away, leaving a four-foot gap to the other side, where the path began again. Zoila leapt across easily, her skirt billowing around her knees in a blue puff. She went on a few paces and then glanced back at me.

"Well?" she demanded.

"My God, Zoila, I can't do it. I really can't this time."

"Then we part," she said. "Good luck on your climb back up. It's about to rain, and it will be more slippery." There was scorn in her voice. She turned and started walking.

I screamed at her, "Zoila, please! Don't desert me like this!" I was crying again, with uncontrollable sobs.

I stood there for several minutes, until I had stopped crying and become calm. I judged the distance and my footing—and leapt across. The thought I held in my mind was "If I fall, I fall." It had a sort of Gertrude Stein ring to it. "How very original, Lynn," I thought. "If I fall, I fall!"

Once across, my knees began to shake like ribbons in the wind. They didn't stop shaking, but I kept going. Ahead of me, Zoila turned around to face me. I expected a pat on the back and a compliment for my courage.

"Come on. That was pathetic. I'm surprised you aren't smashed and mangled somewhere down there." She pointed toward the canyon floor, then turned back to the trail and continued on her way.

Her attitude wounded me deeply. I realized how desperately I wanted her approval. I decided she was right, I was pathetic, for I was crying again. To add to my misery, the trail got even worse. We clung to bushes and jagged pieces of rock. Sometimes my toes edged over a cliff that seemed to drop off into forever. It was steep, uneven, and exceedingly slow going.

We came to a small cave and sat down. I was out of breath and dripping with perspiration. I was still miffed at Zoila and didn't say anything. She looked calm, perhaps a little bored. Sitting there, I realized how stiff I was and how many aches and pains I had. I gazed at the fantastic view across the canyon. The sky was golden. I could see the narrow path spiral upward, and I was amazed that I had managed it. Nearby, a glint of sunlight caught my eye. I stood up, and there on a ledge was a gold Mayan mask inlaid with turquoise, emerald, and jade. The stones were carved in exquisite snake and jaguar designs.

"Zoila, look at these gems and this mask. It's surely solid gold. Do you know why it's here?"

Zoila's voice had a matter-of-fact quality. "It is a beautiful trinket. You take it. It is a gift from the spirits of la caldera."

I climbed up the almost perpendicular ledge and ran my hands over the gleaming surface of the mask, brushing away the dust.

"It's worth a fortune."

"Take it."

"But I can't just take it, Zoila. Maybe it's here for a reason."

"Of course you can. You found it."

"But I simply can't. I don't know why, but I can't."

I took a final look at the gorgeous mask shimmering in the sun. The bright stones glimmered alluringly. I turned away and crawled down from the ledge. The discovery had somehow made me melancholy.

"Zoila, you take it. I just can't."

"Never," Zoila said. "Treasures belong to the one who first sees them."

I shook my head.

"Then move," she said. And she was off once more.

I followed, wondering why I had left such a treasure behind me. Soon I stopped even these thoughts as I began to slip and slide, very nearly falling off the ledge, and in the process managing to wrench my back. The pain shot up my spinal cord.

"Zoila, my back. I've hurt my back."

Zoila stopped and gazed at me in solemn silence. "You look like you might survive," she said cynically.

"Thanks," I mumbled under my breath. My back felt like it had a dagger in it, but I kept going. By now the four edges of the canyon were towering all around us. It was becoming more like we were in a great depression in the jungle floor, created by centuries of running water. The jungle smells of allspice and dark earth blew on the wind. A low mist surrounded the waterfall at the bottom and billowed through the treetops. We were nearing the nadir. The air became even more damp and the trail even more slippery. We walked carefully and soon were enshrouded in the mist. I could barely see Zoila in front of me, and the sound of rushing water was quite loud. I stopped for a moment to sneeze. As I opened my eyes, the mist began to swirl into a funnel, as if assisted by some supernatural power. It seemed to be disappearing down into the middle of an enormous vortex, which was created by a whirlpool on the surface of a river at the bottom of a waterfall. Zoila put her arm around me to steady me.

"Zoila," I said, "we have just walked into a spiral within la caldera, have we not?"

"We have."

"How can there be a river down here at the bottom of this crater?"

"It cuts underground near where we began our descent and comes out over there." She pointed with her walking stick.

"And then where does it go?"

"It goes into the canyon wall over there and is subterranean for many miles. The river comes up out of a mouth of the earth. I will take you there one day if you want to see it."

We descended lower, and I watched in awe as pieces of foam flew up into the air, and logs drifting on the river's edge were caught in the force of the whirlpool, pulled under, and disappeared.

"That is where we come from," Zoila said in my ear. She pointed at the middle of the whirlpool with her stick. "It is to that mystery we are trying to return."

My eyes could bear only so much of looking into the whirlpool. I leaned a little against Zoila for support, feeling clumsy and ungainly. She moved with such grace. We were both dripping wet from the heat and the gathering moisture of mist and spray. I noticed big liquid drops running down the sides of Zoila's face.

She turned to me and said, "See the vanishing point in the

center. That is the void. Watch how a path is created by ripples
spiraling out from the center. You were born of the void, and the
swell is like the outwardness of things. This is like our earth walk. In
our youth and ignorance we walk farther and farther from the
center, until we are very far away from our original nature. That is
how life is. That is its pattern. Most of us live way out on the
perimeter of the spiral. Then, at some point in life, something
special happens to you—an insight, a death, and you begin to
wonder about yourself and ask questions. 'What does life mean?
Where do I come from?' Has this not happened to you?"

"Yes."

"Haven't you wondered why it is difficult to find your true
nature?"

"Yes, I have tried to find my way home."

"Go back to the source. Watch the whirlpool. From such powers
the universe has evolved. The powers of the universe are within you.
See how everything is swallowed into the center? It is ordained that
all be pulled in. The universe will feed into itself, and all creatures
great and small will be liberated."

"Then why is it so difficult for us, Zoila?"

"Because of ignorance and false identity. Come, follow me."

I followed along, and soon we were standing on the canyon floor
at the bottom of the spiraling trail.

"This way," Zoila said.

The ground was wet and swollen, and a swampy area, with the
ground deep and sucking, retarded our progress. Tall reeds were
abundant in all directions. A broad expanse of water plunged and
rumbled from the mouth of a cave to the left. Silvery-green leaves
on great gnarled trees rustled in the wind, standing out starkly
against the backdrop of the dark canyon walls. Golden streams of
sunlight as brilliant as searchlights illuminated the forest. The cliffs
above were dressed in dark shadows, creating puzzling and shifting
images. I was giddy with exhaustion and drank it all in. The canyon
was like a primordial dream, and I was absorbed with the spirit of
the place.

We pushed through some reeds to the edge of the pool beneath the falls. The noise thundered in my ears. We were about twenty-five feet from the whirlpool. I watched branches and a small tree swirl out of sight. Being so close made me shudder.

"Watch carefully, Lynn," Zoila said loudly. "Realize that those branches and that tree are sucked into the center without the slightest effort. Perhaps it is identification with objects and clinging to addictions that keeps you from the source."

I nodded my head in acknowledgment.

After a few moments watching the whirlpool, Zoila said, "Let's walk over there nearer the falls."

Zoila leapt from the stone on which she had been standing to another rock, and then down. She disappeared into a wall of reeds and a bank of mist.

"Wait a minute," I yelled.

I had pursued her for about five paces when I started sinking deeper into the mud and sand. The earth was shifting underneath me, and soon I was up to my knees and stuck.

I screamed for Zoila, but the roar of the falls drowned out my voice. I tried to turn back, but I couldn't even do that. I struggled and sank to my thighs. I screamed again for Zoila until my voice trembled. The situation seemed impossible. At that moment I felt Zoila was a cold and evil woman. There was no compassion in the world. Everything was against me. All I could do was struggle against forces that were out to destroy me. I cursed my fate and Agnes and Zoila. Surely I was not going to die down here in this hidden canyon where no one would care or mourn my passing. The more I struggled the more securely I was held.

After what seemed like an hour, Zoila returned. Her eyes sparkled with amusement, as though she were not at all surprised to see me writhing in the mud and sand. She whistled through her teeth and shook her head. "Well, see what all your fussing and struggling has done."

I tried to straighten up and look dignified. "Zoila, I'm in no mood for a lecture."

"Stand still, and listen to me," Zoila said.

She leapt up on a decayed log and perched like a parrot with her
head cocked to one side.

"You're stuck because you think too much. You think your
knowledge is going to get you out of the mess you're in. You believe
you're going to master the situation with your mind." She chuckled.
"Let me tell you where your mental gymnastics will take you. They
will take you five feet under."

"You didn't have to leave me."

"You have left yourself. You don't listen to your will, and you are
full of fear. Your clinging mind has brought you to this sad state."
She giggled with delight. "Listen to your entirety, Lynn, your total
self."

"I'm trying," I said. I was.

"We have trouble finding our way back to the center of the spiral
because we have enthroned the mind. As long as the mind is the
ruler, you will spend your life stuck in a swamp just as you are now.
You are full of addictions that will strangle you, just as the
quicksand will if you let them dominate. You will lose your luminous
form and your life force. When that happens, it's all over. You're
weak, and you slumber." She laughed.

"I don't think it's funny," I growled.

"But it is funny. The joke is that these addictions prop you up in
a false way, just like the mud with no bottom is propping you up.
The very sands that are destroying you make you feel safe for a
while. Then they begin to suck you under to interminable sleep.
You felt safe down here once you got into the bottom of the
canyon. You didn't notice that you were on a dangerous foundation
and were sinking to your peril. Now you could die. Ponder the
lesson of life. We come here to go back to where we came from.
But our mind tells us that we need props to survive. We believe the
king we have enthroned. We obey him and choose intoxicating
props such as fear of success or fear of failure or fear of death. Or
we don't think we're good enough. You felt that way at the top of
the canyon. You had to be pushed beyond your king's limits to see
that your self-concept was an illusion. That's the addiction you had,
and it kept you from walking down toward your own mystery, your

enlightenment. Just like on the trail. If one addiction doesn't work, you find a new one. You were afraid to jump over the abyss, but you finally did it. And again you overcame your self-imposed limits. When the spirits of la caldera offered you a treasure, you could not avail yourself of it."

"Why couldn't I, Zoila?"

"Because you didn't feel worthy of such riches. And what happened next? You slipped and hurt your back. Do you know why?"

"No."

"Because you're afraid to take your power. It's something worth seeing. You backed away from power, your own power. It sounds simple. You lost your faith in your own capacity. This constriction of energy manifested itself as a stabbing pain in your back."

I began to sob uncontrollably. The moisture from the mist, the spray, and the heat joined my tears and splashed down into the mud. I tried to throw myself forward, but my upper body wouldn't extend. I dangled forward, wracked with spasms. "I'm sorry I didn't do better," I wept.

"And now you're going to punish yourself even more. That's King Brain talking, incessantly talking. You're too hard on yourself. That's a big addiction for many women. King Brain likes to rack you, doesn't he? Your fear of desertion is one of his big whips. Your need for approval. All these addictions leak your power right out of you and make you slumber."

"What can I do, Zoila?"

"You are lucky you have experienced these ordeals, these lessons, for new wisdom is afoot. Be proud of yourself and what you've accomplished. Cease your struggling now. You have ambushed yourself. Sometimes a guide is helpful." She gazed down at me in perfect calmness.

"Will you guide me?" I asked.

Stabbing her staff down into the mud, she hopped down off of the rotten trunk and walked over to me, not sinking more than an inch. I wondered how she could do such a thing.

"Zoila, why aren't you sinking?"

"There's a trick, of course, to walking on this sludge. But it is nothing that can be put into words. It can be realized only in the heart and in the total being." She held out her hand, and I grasped it. "Now don't battle with me. Don't think. Just pull gently on my hand, and let yourself be pulled up and out. The mud will release you if you release it."

I tugged and followed her advice as best I could. Nothing seemed to be happening, no victory of any kind over the powerful quicksand. I was about to give up, when I looked into Zoila's face. I saw an indescribable force in her eyes. There was a sucking sound, and I began to slide free. It almost frightened me, and I grabbed hold of Zoila's arm with my other hand. I was out.

I bounded onto the rotten tree trunk and ran back toward the pool and firmer ground. This time Zoila followed me. When I got to the edge of the water I sat down. I was completely spent, but joyous, as though I had been released from the hold of my own lower energies. Zoila crouched down near me. I was still panting but soon managed to get my breath. We sat in silence for some time, watching the whirlpool.

Zoila took my hand and led me down river. We entered the water at a place where it was less turbulent. Islands of foam and jungle foliage floated by as we waded out waist-deep. She pointed with her walking stick. "See that flat river stone at the bottom of the falls?"

"That one?"

"Yes, she is the seat of Tlazolteatl. With her waters I shall wash the mud from your body."

Slowly, with great care, Zoila washed the mud from my legs. Then, clasping hands and holding them up to the setting sun, we prayed for wholeness and transformation in the water of magicians. We thanked the Goddess and the spirits that had attended us. Then we splashed for a while. Standing up to our waists, we could feel the strength of the current pulling our legs toward the spiraling whirlpool.

The return to Llano was much less precipitous and thankfully so. A fine rain had begun to fall as we went up a zigzagging trail. I hadn't noticed it before. After reaching the top of the rimrock, we headed straight for home and got there just as dusk was settling in.

I went immediately to my hammock, and the next morning I awoke before the sun was up. I was filled with a most peculiar kind of energy; the lethargy I had felt the previous morning was gone. A whole new level of joy was in my heart, and I indeed felt transformed. An extraordinary life spirit was in me, and I felt like prowling and dancing: I felt at one with the cats, the old yellow dog, and the birds that were waking in the trees. I wanted to wander naked in the jungle and become a wild thing living in the trees. I felt a part of the wind and the smells. I did a few dance steps and a twist or two. I saw myself as a huntress along rivers. My hair, the color of yellow grasses, was blowing in the wind, and my nose was nestled in the soft fur of my mate.

I didn't know what to do with all the energy contained within me. I fell back into my hammock and kicked the ground in a slow, rhythmic rocking. The south wind felt like corn silk tickling over my legs. I wondered what would happen if I left everything in Los Angeles and just lived in Llano forever. Life seemed happy and exciting here. Maybe I could just happily exist—just *be*. I was drifting off dreamily into this new life when I heard a familiar laugh.

"I've never seen Lynn smile in her sleep before."

The words snapped me back to consciousness. "Hi, Agnes," I said. The vision had disappeared. I rubbed my eyes. "I've missed you."

Zoila came up next to Agnes and laughingly said, "That's true. I'll bet Lynn has really longed for your return. We went to la caldera yesterday."

Agnes feigned surprise. "Did you enjoy yourself?"

They stared at me until I finally stammered, "Well, I learned a lot."

We all laughed.

I sat up in the hammock and watched the sun shine off the dew drops on the lettuce in Zoila's garden. I felt very relaxed now, and happy with my accomplishment on the spiraling trail of self-realization. I asked for something to eat.

"I'll fix breakfast," Zoila said.

We sat around the food, talking and laughing about my experiences with Zoila. It was obvious I was a very happy woman.

After a short silence I asked, "What has happened to Hyemeyohsts Storm, Agnes? I haven't seen him in such a long time."

"Who is Hyemeyohsts Storm?" Zoila raised her eyebrows.

"Storm is a writer, a breed medicine man who comes from the north." Agnes paused for a moment sipping juice from her gourd cup. "Lynn, your discipline is very different than that of Storm. What you have written about him has been symbolic. This is good; he has taught you the power and use of symbolism and it has enriched your life. There is no longer a need for this experience. You have become a woman of your own power."

I thought about this for a long time, Agnes watching me casually. Finally I said, "But I miss him and the fun we used to have."

"So do I," Agnes said as she and Zoila got up. We cleared the table.

Zoila said, "You look confused Lynn. You're having a problem with literal and symbolic acts."

"Yes, I guess I am trying to understand."

"In the Bible, Jesus lifted up bread and said, 'This is my body.' Then he lifted up a cup of wine and said, 'This is my blood.' These were literal acts with symbolic meaning. Do you see?" Zoila asked.

"Yes, thank you."

Zoila gave me a big hug.

From the tangle of the two
an exchange surprises
the bear and the deer
become a tree

We might see
whole jungles
emerge
from an embrace

Elizabeth Herron
"Suppose"

# Chapter 7
# A Sorcerer's Shadow

Early in the afternoon Agnes announced that she was returning to the hacienda. I was to stay with Zoila.

"Do you want me to walk with you, Agnes?"

"I prefer walking alone." And suddenly she was gone.

Several children were in the house, laughing, fighting, causing a commotion. I had not thought much about Zoila's home life. I knew she was a grandmother, but I had no idea how old she was. As with Agnes and Ruby, she appeared elderly sometimes and then quite young at other times. It seemed to be a natural aspect of these extraordinary women. And their unbounding energy, ordinarily associated with youth, served them well.

"Are these all your grandchildren, Zoila?" I asked, watching a nine-year-old girl named Rosa chasing a chicken out of the room we were in. Rosa stopped in midstride, and the frenzied chicken ran ahead of her, flapping its red and purple wings and squawking loudly. Rosa looked up at me with big, black, button eyes and said, "Hi, Leen," and then resumed her chase.

"She is my daughter Marilia's girl."

"How many daughters do you have?" I asked. Somehow I hadn't thought of Zoila with children, even though she was a grandmother.

"I have seven children, four daughters and three sons. A good number, no? They all have their own families now, and they are all very happy."

Later we weeded in the garden. Zoila had a green thumb and took special care of all of her plants, many of them herbs. She cut some tubular grasses that looked like Mormon tea and then took me inside and showed me how to tie them and hang them up to dry.

"Only for a day," she said. "Then we use them."

We swept the dirt floors and washed the dining table and chairs. I chopped some wood with an ax; the logs were difficult to split. I carried several pails of water from the stream. Zoila told me to take a short rest while she peeled some chilies for dinner. I slept as the late afternoon rain cleared the air. I dreamed of the whirlpool until, feeling its strong pull, I awoke. Zoila was not in her hammock, so I got up and looked around. I saw two people silhouetted against the setting sun, embracing in the doorway. It was Zoila with a man. There was great tenderness and warmth in their movements. I wanted to hide and was surprised that I was blushing. I was slinking into the house, embarrassed, when Zoila called to me.

"Lynn, I want you to meet someone."

Walking around the hammock, I went across the porch and into the yard.

"This is José, my husband."

"But I thought . . . Well, I don't know what I thought. I didn't, I guess."

"*Buenas tardes,*" José said. We shook hands, and he held mine warmly. His palm and fingers were strong and rough from work. He was dressed in loose white pants and shirt, and wore simple leather sandals on his broad, well-shaped feet. His presence delighted me. I stared at his face. His salt-and-pepper hair was neatly combed, and it set off his darkly tanned skin to great advantage.

"Your husband is very handsome," I said.

Zoila elbowed me, giggling. "What's the matter with you, Lynn? You look so startled. Didn't you know I had a husband?"

"I guess not," I mumbled. "Excuse me. I'm delighted to meet you, José."

We went inside the house. José laid down several bundles wrapped in newspaper on the counter, then handed me a small bundle.

I was surprised. "For me?"

He nodded.

Zoila and José watched me carefully untie the white string and unwrap the newspaper. Inside was a small clay hummingbird with outspread wings.

"What a beautiful shape and color!" I said. There was a hole in its pointed beak and another hole in its tail.

José pointed to the clay tail feathers and puckered his lips. "Blow on it," he said.

I held it up to my mouth and blew. A very sweet sound came out, and I was thrilled. I handed it to Zoila to try. She pressed it to her lips and blew several successive notes.

She handed it back. "Hummingbirds seem to come to you," she said.

"The hummingbird is Lynn's little brother," José said. "And your brother is a great warrior. He can lead you to the food that you need to live. Watch him and study his ways." The words were halting and accented, but I could easily understand him. A tranquil but powerful quality to his voice made me instantly alert. My head jerked up, and I gazed into his eyes searchingly. A shiver went through me, like seeing the ocean for the first time. There was an intense power in his eyes and a panther-like wildness. I felt a bond between us, the kind of bond that transcends nationality or blood or family, a binding of magicians of like kind.

"Welcome to our family," he said simply, his eyes shifting from the depth of the Pleiades to a soft twinkle.

He tousled the top of my hair with his hand as if I were a young child, then turned to help Zoila with the packages of supplies he had brought. He slapped her affectionately on the bottom and winked at me. His face brightened with a big smile, and we all laughed and helped prepare chili rellenos for dinner.

Over strong coffee after dinner I began to realize that José and Zoila were like young lovers. Yet they had the respect for each other that is built only through living together a long period of time. José appeared younger than Zoila, but still very protective and thoughtful of her needs. His tender thoughtfulness toward his wife set him

apart from most of the other Spanish and Indian men I had
encountered. I was fascinated by them as individuals and as a
couple, and considered it a privilege to be in their company. My
thoughts must have shown on my face, because Zoila kept staring at
me oddly, then spoke.

"When I met José forty years ago, he thought he wanted to be a
garage mechanic. I was already a *curandera*, because my
grandmother was the best and most effective *curandera* from Solola
in Guatemala. She raised me and taught me everything she knew
about mountain spirits and plants. She knew the hidden designs of
nature and the eternal fires within all things. She knew many things,
and she helped me move toward totality. She shared with me her
beauty and peace.

"José and I fell in love on St. Jerome's feast day, but his family
was afraid of me. José was ten years younger than me, and I was a
healer. His mother was serious and strong, and she put up a terrible
stink. José did not want to offend his madre, so he left me and went
to Mérida to work on trucks. I was very hurt, and I married
someone else. This man was a drunk and a bad man, and I ran him
off after our first child was born. I could take care of myself. Then I
heard that José had been taken very ill with hepatitis and fever, and
was dying. He had lost his will to live."

"So what happened?" I asked.

"His mother and father brought him to me to cure. His mother
wanted to know how much it would cost. I talked with her a long
time that day after I had prepared medicines and herbs for José. I
made her see that in wanting her own prestige she had destroyed
her son. Her greed and self-importance was blinding her to her son's
wish for happiness. I explained to her that this was the reason that
he might not live. She was angry and didn't want to believe me, but
then she said a strange thing. She said that she would rather he
would die than be stolen by another woman. She was so shocked by
her own words that she cried. I treated her. She gave her consent,
and José and I were married. She and I became friends after a
while."

I shook my head slowly and started to comment on Zoila's story.

José held up his hand and said, "But that was only the beginning. I nearly died in a coma. That I am alive today is due entirely to Zoila's remarkable gifts. I had many strange dreams, and she helped me with the plants to cross over into the mystery. I know now it was shaman's sickness, and she healed me there. She taught me many things."

"What did she teach you?"

José smiled. "She taught me how to be alive."

"During your illness? But you were nearly dead."

"Exactly. And in more ways than you can count. I was in love with Zoila from the moment I saw her, but my family were strict Catholics, and I was afraid of their disapproval. I had to almost die to find my way back to her and to my true self. I had always been able to see people and what was troubling them. I wanted to be a *curandero,* but my family thought that was wrong and the mark of the devil. Besides, there was no one to instruct me." José smiled at Zoila.

Zoila poured coffee into our gourd cups and then said, "My grandmother always told us that it was much better for women to marry men that are younger, because men tend to die twelve to sixteen years earlier than women. Of course, in Mexico women often get married in their early teens, and that makes life difficult. Sometimes the customs of a people should be changed. I have many women friends who spend the last years of life without a husband to share it. That's a tragedy. It's those years when you could especially enjoy a husband."

"I was lucky to find Zoila," José said. He had listened to the discussion carefully while leaning back in his chair. Then he commented, "I have been gone a lot these past few years because people have heard of us. People far away need me."

"Don't you miss him, Zoila?"

"Him? I can't wait until he packs his suitcase." She looked at José and smiled. Their eyes held for a moment, and I could sense the complete understanding and alliance between them. She turned back to me and continued. "When people marry, they usually begin to

live each other's lives. At that point the reason for living is buried
forever."

"What do you mean?"

"José and I have come onto this earth walk to learn very different
lessons. I have instructed him, so we are both healers. But that
doesn't matter. He works differently than I do and uses different
powers. Because we both need freedom to grow we are apart a great
deal of the time.

"José is also an apprentice to our everyday world. He is an
apprentice to the fields and helps raise and harvest the crops of
henequen, as I work to raise the corn. Let no one doubt it. There is
a great need for balance between substance and spirit.

"Many people want to become *curanderos.* What a pity they rush
off into the shaman land of the *curandero* without tending to their
home fires first. Here we are speaking of foundations. If people
follow their whims, spirit is not manifested on the earthly plane,
where we need it most.

"It's all well and good for a *curandero* to function well on the
stomping grounds of the magician. But those who cannot function
well on a day-to-day physical level at some point will have to return
to start over in bitter disappointment. If I were to say, 'José, we
must have a routine in our lives like your mother did,' he would
shrivel up and die. His mother was like Chicomecoatl, the Great
Mother. Remember her in la Ultima Madre ceremony?"

I nodded in recognition.

"She is the authoritative nurturer who sets her life by schedules
and known things. José and I aren't like that. We want to dream
and inspire people to health and well-being. We live for the most
part in unknown worlds. If I were like his mother, with the desire to
always hold up the clock, I would have to learn to honor the
difference between us and let him be. I would have to learn to love
him unconditionally. That's not the easiest thing for nurturing
mothers to do. They tie a lot of strings on their love."

I poured myself another gourd full of coffee and thought about
what Zoila had said. "I found marriage very difficult, because no one
needed what I had to give."

Zoila chuckled. "And your husband didn't understand your needs either, did he?"

"Not at all."

"You see," Zoila asserted, "it is told that in the old culture of the Maya, women and men were taught like you were the other night. They were taught about the translation of Mother Earth's energy, and also about the female energy and how it reveals itself in a person. When we understand the great mothers in us, we can live in harmony and help fulfill each other's destinies."

"I believe many of the women in my culture have turned their backs on femininity," I said.

"That's a great sorrow for our Madre." Zoila touched the dirt floor with the palms of her hands. "If women cannot assume their totality, as feminine, beautiful women, then men will never learn of their female side, and the earth will remain in great disharmony. Women say that it is the men who have created the imbalance on our Mother Earth. It is the men who have conjured our wars. But it is the women's fault. We have permitted it. Men and women need each other; we need to learn from each other. That's part of what this life is all about."

"What do men teach women?" I asked. "Isn't there an exchange between them?"

"Very broadly speaking, men teach women how to organize their consciousness, especially out in the everyday world. Women teach men about the sacred dream, how to receive and implement the wisdom of their consciousness. Women teach men how to live. Men teach women how to express their dreams, and bring an exchange of energy back from the world, such as money or food or other material goods."

"But I see a lot of women make money without men," I said, straightening myself in the chair.

Zoila turned to José and then back to me. "Yes, women today can earn money, but only if their man shield is well developed. If a woman is weak in her man shield, she will give and give and demand nothing in return. She will become a martyr. A man can teach a woman about that in many ways."

We were silent a while. I could see that José was very tired. He had returned home from a long journey. Gratitude was in my heart for the fate that had brought me into the presence of these two superb people. I helped clean the table and wash the bowls. I excused myself and said that it was getting late, and I had better be returning to the hacienda. José offered to accompany me through the jungle, but I declined.

"Don't forget your hummingbird flute," Zoila said.

We all embraced.

"And watch out for pumas," José said.

I laughed as I walked away. Several yards distant I turned to look back. José and Zoila stood in the doorway with their arms around each other. We waved, and I continued on. The sky was vast and full of stars. My sandals crunched into the gravel of the dirt road. As I passed through the village of Llano I felt lighthearted and very touched by the obvious love between Zoila and José.

Human sounds seemed to carry farther than usual that night. I could hear laughter in the village. I was walking at a quick stride. For no apparent reason I felt a tingling sensation shoot through my body. I looked up just in time to see a shadow the size of a huge devilfish float off into the nearest treetop and disappear. I was certain I hadn't imagined it. My eyes darted around searching for the cause of this strange phenomenon. A cool wind had come up out of the underbrush and I wrapped my flowered shawl more closely around my shoulders. The birds and the creatures of the night were entirely quiet; it was the same sort of quiet that settles in before an earthquake.

I walked very quickly, imagining all sorts of spooky things. It was the presence of Red Dog that I had sensed. I was in complete terror by the time I had gone through the jungle and arrived at the hacienda. I ran up the stairs and opened the door to the room. Agnes greeted me. My chest was still heaving.

I immediately asked, "Could Red Dog turn himself into a shadow that hovers above you and looks like a devilfish? And could he quiet all the animal sounds of the night?"

Agnes looked at me curiously, "Why do you ask?"

"Because, Agnes, that's what just happened."

"*What* happened? You're not explaining yourself very well."

I explained as best I could exactly what had occurred.

Agnes was amused by my severe discomfort and patted my hand. "Red Dog has many guises. I don't know what kind of flyer that was you saw. If it was Red Dog, you can be thankful it was just reconnaissance and not an attack. Don't let it disturb you. Next time he'll probably kill you, and it'll be all over."

"Agnes!" I said, stomping my foot.

"By and by you are going to meet with him face-to-face, you know. He's afraid of you now, but that will make him all the more formidable. I'll hate to lose you, but you are a weak, defenseless female."

"Agnes!"

"Sooner or later," she said, shaking her head.

"You better be with me, Agnes."

She cocked an eyebrow. "Get some sleep."

After a bath I crawled into bed and turned out the light. I stared at the dark wood vigas and thatch of the ceiling. I talked about José and love and relationships until I realized Agnes was snoring. I soon fell asleep.

The sources
And the crude bone
    —we say
*Took place*
Like the mass of the hills.
'The sun is a molten mass'. Therefore
Fall into oneself—?
Reality, blind eye
Which has taught us to stare—

                George Oppen
                   "Route"

# Chapter 10
# The Face of the Earth

Early in the morning Agnes and I made our way down the deserted road behind the hacienda. The early morning sun was creamy white and still low on the horizon. As we walked, I took sips of tea from a small hollow gourd that I held carefully with both hands in front of me. It was a long stretch of road, and I felt supremely happy. Everything seemed wonderful. Even the gourd cup seemed so much better than a regular cup. Surely it contained life as well as hot liquid.

The sun got higher and streamed down over my shoulders and was beginning to warm the hard-packed earth of the road. As usual, a light rain had fallen during the night. The puddles of muddy water were beginning to dry. I saw fruit trees and could smell the smoke from burning fires in the henequen fields.

"Feel that sun," I said. "Doesn't it feel exhilarating?"

"The light that you are feeling now is life that died to its mother some time ago. When you break a tooth or have your hair cut, those pieces of yourself are dead to you forever. Does the sun appear to change, or do you feel any different when your hair ends fall away as they are cut?"

"Well, no. Not really."

"The other day you asked me to speak of death, and this is as good a time as any. When your spirit parts from your body, it is the same, the final giveaway. Your spirit continues to emanate light and strength like the sun, but it then chooses a different way to be seen. That is all death is, you see."

Several colorful birds darted and maneuvered swiftly in the air above us. They kept their distance but continued to put on a display for us.

"I understand, Agnes."

"No, you don't understand, or you would never be afraid of death."

"Well, I wish I understood," I said.

Agnes turned and laughed. "If you understood your death you would be happy, happy with everyone and everything that came in front of you. You see the beautiful birds flying, and they make you happy. But what if they were airplanes dropping murder out of the sky? You wouldn't like it. But I tell you honestly, if we did see airplanes sent to destroy us, I would be just as happy as you are looking at those winged creatures."

"Agnes, that's insane."

"No, you're insane, always holding on to everything, especially your fear. If you understand life, then when you lose it, maybe it won't be so bad. If you were to lose your father, or your dog, Muffin —is that his name?"

"Yes."

"Anything at all. All of your attachments. You won't understand this either. But your children, your dog, your car, your house, your clothes, your objects—they're all dead fingernails. Essential life and love can never leave you, because you are that."

The birds were flying directly overhead now, not a dozen feet from the ground, making chattering and chirping sounds. Even though I couldn't understand Agnes's asserted ability to be jubilant in the face of sudden oblivion, I felt especially in tune with the earth. The view of the slowly sloping hillside with clusters of towering trees under an awning of clear blue sky was fascinating. The dirt road we were on started winding lazily through the valley. For half an hour we trudged along, side by side, until Agnes suggested we stop and rest.

We both lay back in clumps of high grass at the side of the road,

forming a sort of makeshift nest. Agnes gave me a drink of water
from a gourd canteen, and when I handed it back to her after
taking several swallows, a yellow butterfly landed on my finger. It
didn't fly away when Agnes took the canteen from my hand. I held
it up to the sunlight, examining the brilliant butter-colored wings. I
tried to kiss it, but it flew away. I watched as it hopped and floated
on the air. For some reason that creature conjured up images of the
undulating movement of the sea and then of galloping horses in a
field.

Agnes was studying my face. She held her gaze on me for several
seconds and said, "Today is a special day for you."

"Special? How so?"

"You might learn something today. Who knows?"

"I try to learn something every day," I said, a bit indignantly.

Agnes laughed.

"Well, I do," I insisted.

This set her to laughing even harder, until tears were rolling down
her face, and she said, "Lynn, Lynn, stop! You're too brittle.
Learning something isn't the matter of great importance you may
think." She brushed away the tears from her eyes. Sitting with a
huge grin on her face, she said, bursting into laughter once more,
"It's knowing that's important."

"I don't see how you can know something without first learning
it."

"Good point," she said.

I didn't know how she had managed it, but Agnes had completely
spoiled my mood. I tried to look around at the scenery, but I was
seeing with different eyes.

"Teach me something," Agnes said. "I try to learn something
every day, no matter who I'm with. I'm serious, Lynn. Teach me
something."

She said it so earnestly and casually, I believed her.

"Well, what would you like me to teach you, Agnes?"

"Something you know."

Agnes hadn't played this cat-and-mouse game with me for quite
some time, and I was determined to get the best of her for once. I

racked my brain trying to think of something that Agnes didn't
know. I couldn't think of anything. I knew how to mix an extra dry
martini, but that would sound foolish. I knew how to make a lion's
meal of bouillabaisse. That too seemed out of place. I was an expert
horsewoman, but Agnes made me look like a tinhorn. I'd seen her
do the most incredible things with horses, things I'd never be able
to duplicate.

"I'm waiting," Agnes said.

"I'm still thinking."

"Think no more. Sometimes it's a waste of time. I'll tell you
what. For the next few days, you be the teacher and I'll be the
apprentice."

"I don't know if I want to do *that,* Agnes."

"Don't be silly. I'm the apprentice waiting for some sage advice
from my great teacher, Lynn. I'm waiting for any crumb you might
throw a hungry intellect."

"Are you sure you want to be my apprentice, Agnes?"

"Absolutely."

"You won't get mad and take it out on me later?"

"You know me better than that."

"It might be fun. Let's try it."

"OK, let's go. By the way, where are we going?"

"For a walk."

For the next four days the usual order of business was reversed. I
taught Agnes everything I could think of that I might know and she
didn't. I taught her about Arabian horses and their bloodlines from
Egypt and about the Tibetan Book of the Dead. I must say she was
a diligent student. She took notes, did everything I told her to the
letter, questioned me incessantly. She never complained of harsh
treatment when I made her sweep the room or make beds or run
errands. At the end of the fourth day I was stumped. I couldn't
think of any further useful knowledge I could impart to Agnes that
she didn't already know.

That night before going to bed, I said, "This is too big a
responsibility, Agnes."

"Yes, I believe you have worn yourself down."

"It's very difficult being a teacher. You really have to organize your information."

"Good, you've learned that."

"And you're an excellent student, Agnes. When I asked you to repeat things back to me, you embarrassed me. You remembered them almost verbatim."

"Good. So you've learned what it is to be a worthy apprentice."

"I certainly have. But I feel badly about the quality of my teaching skills."

"Much to the contrary. You are an excellent teacher. You surprised me." She winked. "I've never understood the depth of your experiences and knowledge until now. I've learned much that may be useful to me, especially if I ever come to Los Angeles for a visit. I would say that as my teacher you rank about four stars."

"Thank you, Agnes," I said. "But do you mind taking over? I realize more than ever now why I am your apprentice."

"Do I have to?" Agnes said. "I was just starting to enjoy it."

"You have to."

With that we hugged and went to bed. Even in the dark I saw the gleam in Agnes's eyes. Now it was my turn to laugh and finally understand the profundity of her sly humor. I had many dreams that night, and when Agnes woke me the next morning there was no doubt in my mind that she had resumed command.

"Get your medicine bundle and your pipe," Agnes said once my eyes had adjusted to the morning light. "We are going somewhere. I want you to drive us there at once."

I got up, shook the stiffness out of my limbs, and got ready to leave the hacienda. We went down and had some breakfast and soon were on the road. Instead of going to Zoila's, we went deeper into the jungle.

"Park the car," Agnes said after we had driven a few miles.

I pulled over and parked.

"Bring your things."

I got my medicine bundle and pipe bag out of the back seat and hurried to catch up with Agnes. She was walking hurriedly down a jungle path, brushing away ferns and vines. We crossed a small

stream, still following the path. The vegetation was getting wilder all
the time. Agnes was going so fast that I was starting to get winded.
We came into a clearing of many fields. A small adobe thatch roof
house was in the distance. Agnes headed straight for it.

"What now?" I said.

It was almost noon when we reached the house. We pushed our
way through the wooden door. The house that had appeared
deserted was full of people. Zoila and José were there and several
women I had seen at the hacienda. Two young men were standing
in front of the group, alongside Zoila and José. They were told to
join the rest, and they sat down. Zoila and José also sat down.
Agnes immediately joined the group. I felt self-conscious and
wondered what kind of meeting it was.

Zoila motioned for me to come over and sit on a grass mat
opposite her. There was a murmur of whispered conversation and
then a hush as I did so. I noticed that the dirt floor between Zoila
and myself had been smoothed, and many of her bundles lay there
on a large piece of lace. Zoila smiled at me, sensing my
uncomfortableness.

José stood up. He began addressing the group in his native
Mayan. I couldn't understand any of it, but he soon had the entire
room in an absolute uproar. He made funny faces, saluted, shrugged,
and winked. It was obviously some sort of comedy routine.

Zoila saw the apprehension and astonishment written on my face.
I laughed louder than anyone as José stepped on burning copal and
hopped around the room on one foot, clutching the other as though
he had third degree burns, and hooting like an owl.

Very softly Zoila said to me, "Be aware of the rhythms in this
room. It is important that everyone laughs. We won't begin this
teaching until everyone is happy."

José caught Zoila's eye and made obscene gestures at her. She
started to giggle. He was a hilarious clown, and now I couldn't stop
laughing. I wondered what kind of gathering this could be.
Obviously it was a sacred meeting because Zoila had brought her
most sacred bundles, as had I. Watching José's clowning, I thought
of how desperately serious the search for truth often becomes, and

the smug rapture seen on the studiously solemn faces of devotees of
so many disciplines.

"These people are apprentices and are involved in one way or
another with our work," Zoila said. "So I have gathered them to sit
and lend their power to the mesa, the mask, the face of the earth—
what you call an altar. From the earth a tree with many branches
will grow. I think there will be something in it for you if you want."
She said something in Mayan, and everyone laughed.

"What did you say, Zoila?"

She turned back to me, grinning. "I said I wanted them to see
how stupid a gringo can be."

I laughed and didn't think of it as an unkind statement. I
adjusted myself so I was comfortable on the mat. Zoila began
tracing a rectangle on the dirt floor with a pointed stick. She drew a
cross through it, which sectioned it off into four pyramids, their
apexes meeting in the center.

Zoila spoke first in Mayan and then in English. "Now this is the
form that many altars take. They are usually used by our sisters in
the south and southeast. Most often, on the left side is death. On
the right side is life. Death and life can be interpreted as negative
and positive, or evil and good. Every altar is similar and yet
different, because every shaman is different. We all have our
individuality."

She pointed with her stick. "On this top mesa, or top triangle if
you prefer, is the gatherer pyramid. It essentially brings in power
and holds it. Because of this you place antennalike objects there—
candles, canes, sticks, feathers, prayer sticks—whatever pulls energy
down from the universe and into your prayers."

Zoila pointed again. "The bottom triangle is your personal giving
of power toward the center, where the pyramids converge and meet.
Your shooting crystals go here, as well as your personal arrows. Your
most powerful givers of power go here."

She nodded toward the center. "In the center of any mesa goes
your translator. This is your hermaphrodite or androgynous power
representative. This object is neither good nor evil, neither positive
nor negative."

Zoila looked up, and my concentration was broken. José was at it again. He had slipped into one of Zoila's dresses unseen and was curtsying to various members of the group, including Agnes! He tried to kiss one of the young men. Everyone howled at his antics. He suddenly stood perfectly still.

When everyone had quieted down, Zoila said first in Mayan and then in English, "Like José, is that a man or a woman?" I peered at him through the billowing copal smoke. I was about to laugh, when I saw Agnes out of the corner of my eye moving up behind me. Using both hands, she grasped my head and turned it to where I could stare only at José. I didn't know what this was supposed to accomplish, but as I steadily watched him he took on a softened look. His form started to blur and then go back into focus. His features seemed to lift out of themselves. His mouth became female, full and sensual, and he appeared to have voluptuous breasts and a narrow-waisted, curvaceous body. I tried to regain my sense of perspective but to no avail.

Agnes released me. José was now a woman if ever I'd seen one, flirting outrageously with one of the two young men in the room, eyes blinking demurely, giving him a come-hither look. The young man watched adoringly. The whole thing was so convincing I thought they might go off together into the bushes. Everyone was sharing a bottle of liquor and some smoke.

Zoila waited for quiet. "The hermaphrodite in the center of your altar is the heart. It is to be used to work with positive or negative situations as they arise. It helps you translate any kind of energy into something useful. It is your place of focus. It represents what you are in the most sacred part of yourself."

One of the young men asked a question.

"The question asked," Zoila said, "has to do with an explanation of the center or the hermaphrodite. He wants further elaboration." She spoke to the group in Mayan for several minutes and then turned back to me. "If you were a Catholic, your center would probably be a crucifix. For you, Lynn, it might be your pipe or a crystal from your sacred mountain, a mountain that gives you life force. Your hermaphrodite must be something that can focus your sacred abilities. In a certain sense, it is all that you are."

"I don't understand how a crucifix could be used in both positive and negative situations," I said.

"If a person came to you and believed that an evil spell had been put on her, you would work with your crucifix to center your attention and power on the negative or death side of your altar."

"How?"

"Your crucifix would help you find the item—and there are many —that would assist you. You might use a kidney stone, and through its telling energy be able to find the stone that had been put inside of her by, say, a witch or an enemy. Then you would suck it out of her if that were your way. But that is not your way. You devote yourself to healing the mind and the heart. You would assist a person before or after a healing so that she would not choose to have a stone or a problem again. So the things that you would collect for your altar would be things to do with seeing more clearly —pieces of comets, crystals, power objects from other shamans, and so forth."

I nodded my head that I at least partially understood.

All of a sudden José took hold of my shoulder. At first I started to fight him off, but then I went with it. He was still wearing Zoila's dress, and he was biting and sucking my shoulder. Everyone started to ooh and ah and cheer. Then I felt something give way underneath the skin where he was sucking. José got to his feet, his cheeks puffed out. He spit a tiny clay pot into his hands. Presumably it had been inside me.

"I'm glad I got this before the poison leaked out," José said, wiping his brow. "How do you feel now?" He dumped an inky gray substance out of the pot into his hand and mumbled, "Very bad."

My shoulder had been hurting for several days, and now it didn't. I felt relief. I moved my shoulder up and down. José sat down, crossed his legs, and pretended to be filing his nails. A great commotion of laughter and clapping rang through the house.

"Zoila, my shoulder had been hurting, but it doesn't hurt a bit now."

Zoila smiled. I looked at José, who was going through an

elaborate ritual of putting on lipstick. I couldn't believe my eyes. He was so dainty. I knew he was simply having fun at my expense, or was he? His eyes evaded mine, but then he looked directly at me. For a split second I was transfixed. It was like the meeting of a tiger and a wolf, and then the instant melted. Zoila was speaking to me, but my attention was gone. I could feel a comforting warmth in my shoulder. Zoila gently put her hand on mine, and I realized I was shaking. She offered me a sip of juice from a gourd bowl, which I took.

"Better, no?" she asked.

I had been expecting the pain to come back into my shoulder but it didn't.

"Much better," I said, nodding my head affirmatively.

Zoila studied me. "I work to heal the mind and the heart just like you do," she said. "While I work with you, José watches. He can see the dark places, where your life force is immobile. He can see what has been shot into you or what has been put there by bad persons. He spotted that clay pot in your shoulder and simply sucked it out. In time the poison would have seeped out, and you would have been a very sick woman. Now you have nothing to fear."

"Where did it come from?"

"A female enemy. Actually she could have been your good enemy. With swift eyes you might have seen her, and you could have protected yourself."

There was a wave of laughter. José was balancing the clay pot on his nose, then throwing it up like a seal a foot or so in the air and catching it on his tongue. He then repeated the feat, catching it back on his nose.

"How can someone be a good enemy? Who did this to me?"

"She's a blower with a dark wind for an ally. She must be someone who has a sharp but small tongue, because the pot is so small."

"Does it help me to know this?"

"Surely. Maybe you can recognize her next time. It may be someone you think is a friend, but she fools your eyes. Some enemies are good, because they hurt us when we least expect it and where we are most weak. For you, it is your sensitivity, your feelings. You need to get tougher, and a good enemy hardens you up. She makes you polish your shields."

When Zoila finished speaking, I noticed the light in her serene brown eyes. Despite the serenity, there was an aggressiveness about her eyes. They were definitely loving eyes, but they were unwavering. I wondered if this were the quality she was trying to define. I was getting tired of being told that I had to get tougher. But the alternative seemed to be getting wounded over and over, and I was even more tired of that.

"So what do I do, Zoila?"

"Keep your good enemy until either she changes, or you become stronger."

Softly I said, "Oh, great."

José whirled around and tossed the clay pot to me off the end of his nose. I caught it and was stunned to find that it was as cold as an ice cube. It started to numb my hand, and I set it down. Agnes whispered in my ear for me to watch it carefully. I watched it melt quickly away, dissolve into the dirt floor, and then disappear totally. I was astonished.

"José has melted it with his humor," Zoila said.

The room exploded with clapping and excited talk.

I sat back on my mat, my eyes still wide with wonder. José handed me a small cloth pouch.

"Here," he said, pointing. "Where the pot melted, take that earth, and put it in the pouch."

I scraped up the earth with a gourd Zoila handed me and carefully poured it in and tied the pouch with two pieces of string. I set it with my things.

Zoila got up quickly and chased a white chicken that had wandered inside. She hurriedly came back and sat down. She lifted the pouch in the palm of her hand and said, "Put this pouch on the negative side of your altar. When someone comes to you who has a deceitful mother-in-law or has been the victim of gossip, work with that dirt. It will give you power and understanding to know how best to heal her."

Agnes and José passed around bowls of dried fruit and sunflower seeds. José lit up a cigar and blew acrid puffs of smoke on everyone present. Zoila filled gourd cups with wine and handed them out. One of the young men started to play an ethereal tune on his clay flute. The other young man started to play on a short log drum with the palms of his hands. The sound was deeply reverberating. Every now and again José, who was tending to the needs of those present, struck a round, flat drum that hung from a rafter. He struck the drum with a short stick, adding a nice counterpoint to the other drum. Women began to chant. The music was very strange and lovely.

I chewed on a dried apricot and examined a log-shaped drum that lay flat on the ground. A serpent was carved on one end and an eagle on the other. José, noticing my interest, squatted down next to me.

"That is a split drum," he said, "a *teponaztli*. The two carvings represent the marriage of earth and sky. The world has forgotten the sounds of our Mayan culture. So many of the ancient instruments were lost. My friend Pazatl makes these old songs come alive. It is said that we need humility to hear the voices of nature. Listen to how simple this music is. Nature needs only three instruments to make a storm: lightning, thunder, and rain." With that, he stood up and placed a long piece of bamboo by my ear. "Close your eyes," he said. The music stopped, except for the soft notes of the flute and occasional muted drumbeats. The bamboo next to my ear produced a sound like that of rushing water, first low, then stronger, and I wondered if I would soon be swallowed by a tidal wave. I opened my eyes and realized that the bamboo was closed off on each end, and the sound was produced by pebbles rushing from one end to the other.

"All this beautiful music wakes up the spirits," Zoila said. "They sleep and wait for us to come and entice them to waken. That's why I sing and say beautiful things to my spirits, just like I say beautiful things to José so he will like me."

I looked at José, who had changed clothes and was back to being his handsome male self. I shifted my glance back to Zoila.

"Spirits need to recognize you, Lynn," she continued. "You have to have a name, so they can call to you from their world. Most of the spirits live in the cieba trees, water, and in the mountains. That is why I usually work outside. I believe we have helped you considerably. Now you need to learn the landscape of the face of the earth, which is like a battery."

"A battery?"

"Yes, it builds and holds life force, depending on how powerful your bundles are and depending on how well you can focus your power. My face of the earth, my altar, is different from this altar." She motioned toward her drawing and then erased it with the flat of her hand. Next she drew another rectangle, this one nearly square. Then she drew a circle around the drawing and wrote the words *North, South, East, and West* in English around the outside of the circle. She drew a large X through the quadrangle and a little box on each of the four arms of the X.

"These arms mark the spring, summer, fall, and winter solstices," she said, placing a small circle at the north of the altar. "This is North Wind. He is bald, blind, mean, and the strongest of all winds."

She made another small circle in the south. "This is South Wind. He is a warrior wind. He is good."

She made a heavy circle in the center.

"This is the zenith. This is the place of the man who stands in the middle. He is a hermaphrodite. He is crazy and strong. For La Sabia, a woman of knowledge, the hermaphrodite is also Crazy Woman. We move clockwise around the face of the earth with the sun. Crazy Woman has the perfect balance of the hermaphrodite. She has the power and insight of the ometeotl, the divine duality. Remember that in Mesoamerica the women own water. The sky is male and the earth is female. The south, west, and north are dry and female. The north and east are wet and male. This may seem contradictory and strange, but that is the way it is. The moon lives in the ocean, and the sun lives in the ocean and comes up over the mountain. The sun is the child, husband, and father of the moon. You must understand the movement of the sun and the moon, the

time of the solstices, and the movement of the stars. You see,
everything in the shaman's world is based on the zenith, and this is
especially true of the altar and pyramids."

"I'm having trouble following you, Zoila. Please wait a minute,
because I'm completely confused."

Zoila shifted subtly on her mat. She looked at José, who nodded
his head, and then she dismissed everyone. Each person thanked her
before leaving the hut. Once this was done, José and Agnes peered
over Zoila's shoulder to see what was happening. Sunlight from a
high open window illuminated the patch of dirt floor we were
working on. I tried to start over at the beginning by pointing to a
circle. Zoila read my mind.

"No, that's the summer solstice," she said.

"Then this must be winter," I said.

"That's right."

We went over everything once more, pointing and gesturing to
the diagram. Toward the end of her painstaking recap, I was
beginning to get a feeling for the movement of the seasons and her
world, the world of *La Sabia*—a woman of knowledge. The zenith
and the idea of the hermaphrodite fascinated me most.

"This is most unusual, Zoila," I said. "Much different from
anything I've ever been exposed to. I think I like the concept of the
divine duality the best."

"This is not a concept. You have a tendency to think of ideas as
concepts. As long as you continue this, you will experience only
appearances and not recognize the practical usages. The
hermaphrodite represents the balance of all that is, like a point in a
fulcrum. But remember, he's crazy too, and this is the reason he can
shape the world in new ways."

"It's a most beneficial, well, whatever it is, not concept."

Zoila laughed. "I'll give you another example," she said. "In the
Mayan way there are thirteen holy trees, but the center tree is the
weakest. It's a paradox that it is also the most powerful. The
dumbest is the most wise, says the wise man. Or is it the dumbest?
Agnes has told me of her way, the way of the contrary or sacred
clown. In a clown's craziness, she can be obscene or test any of the

existing structures and ideas to see if they are true and real—and
she gets away with it. She herself is weak, but her very weakness is
her power."

"Is it like the sacred clown who rides backward into battle with a
broken, twisted lance? He has such a profound connection with the
Great Spirit that he totally trusts that he will be unharmed. From a
rational point of view he is a fool."

"I've never heard of that before, but it sounds very similar.
Perhaps it is more understandable if I use the example of the last
child, for she is the last moon. She doesn't fit because she's odd or
abnormal, and yet she knows everything. The Lord of the Shaking
Earth, or Lord of the Earthquakes in your language, is a last child.
He is an idiot and walks crookedly, but he is most powerful." She
looked at me with a curious expression I couldn't read. José and
Agnes were also staring. Then I realized they wanted to know if I
understood.

"I think I do," I finally said.

Zoila said, "I think you have had enough information about the
altar for one day. Tomorrow morning we will begin again. I will
show you how to lay out your mask of the earth and then it will be
more clear to you. This knowledge is as slippery as a fish and
difficult to grasp. Tonight there are still more lessons for you to
learn. For now, let's return to my house."

We got everything that Zoila wanted to take back and then
walked through the jungle to my car. I drove everyone to Zoila's.
We ate a leisurely dinner. Agnes and José went off for a walk
together and left Zoila and I alone.

"This evening it is important for you to establish a connection
with your own star. You will need this experience tomorrow." Zoila
got up from the table. "I just noticed something."

She went into the other room and returned with a bundle.
Unwrapping it, she chose a small, smooth stone and rubbed it over
my shoulder again and again. My shoulder was aching once more,
and also my neck—from driving, I thought. Zoila spoke under her
breath and then held the stone to her forehead.

"Ah!" she finally said. "Foolish telephones."

"What? Telephones?"

"The telephone is one of the reasons you have a sore neck and shoulder. Stop using the telephone."

"You're right, Zoila. I always crook my neck around the receiver. How in the world did you know that?"

"I use this tool. It is my sun stone. I put it on your illness and looked over your body. Then I looked into my stone to see what was wrong with you. I want you to go outside into the fields and find your own sun object, a stone that speaks to you, one you feel you can work with. This stone will stand for your star, your own sunlight."

She gestured, and I got up. I saw that Agnes and José had been watching behind me all along.

"Go now," Agnes said, "while there is still a bit of sunshine. I hear a stone calling to you."

I left the house immediately. Zoila's old yellow dog lazily followed me out into the fields toward the reedy stream. I crossed a ridge of gold and green. My mind was whirling with the day's teachings. With every step I took over the stony ground I felt like I was treading on a mask of the earth. The land flattened out, and I was at least three hundred yards away from the house. I stopped and looked up through patches of leafy green, the sun blinding me for a moment, and then walked out into the field.

The sky was blue and the air was perfectly warm and still. An orange and purple sunset flamed in the west. I sat down near a ditch and thought for a moment of the ancient Mayan teachings of the zenith. I took a few deep breaths and tried to attune myself to the movements of the stars. Suddenly I was startled by what sounded like the faint cry of a child. The sound became louder and turned into a moan. The old yellow dog was digging furiously in a furrow. I got up and walked over. He was quite intent, his muzzle pushed into a hole. I knelt down beside him and stroked his back. He dug some more and then clamped onto something with his teeth. His tail was wagging vigorously. He tried to run away and not let me see what he had found.

"Here, boy!" I called. "Let's see what you've got."

He stopped and reluctantly came to me. I guessed that he had found a long-buried bone. Very carefully, and with a precise and graceful movement of his head, the dog lifted his muzzle straight up toward the setting sun and then gently deposited a small object in my outstretched hand. He sat down and barked, waiting for me to reward him. I leaned over and hugged him and fondled his ears, all the while feeling the object I was clutching in my left hand. It felt odd. Finally I pulled away from the dog to look.

It was small, oblong, and encrusted with dirt. I rubbed the dirt away and, to my shock, sitting in my palm was a perfectly carved stone goddess figure that appeared to me to be from the Olmec period. The figure was carved from a white stone and sparkled in the sun. I rubbed it some more and examined it carefully. It was exquisitely beautiful.

"My own piece of sunlight," I said joyfully. "My own sun stone."

I held her up to the flaming sunset and thanked the powers for bringing us together. I searched around for other antiquities but found nothing else. I took some tobacco from my pocket, sprinkled it in a circle around the hole, and then covered it up, saying a prayer. I ran all the way back to the house. The yellow dog followed at my heels, barking excitedly. I was jubilant.

That night the yellow dog slept with me under a mosquito netting. I was lying face upward, my head on a pillow, and I could look up into the depths of the night sky, a panorama of twinkling stars. The Milky Way seemed vast and overpowering in its intensity. Comets flared. The crescent moon cut with an awesome brightness into the deep purple firmament.

I held the goddess figure clutched to my breast. Zoila had told me that she was my earth star as well as my sun stone, and to pray and be in contact with her before I slept, so she would be in my dreams. When she had handed the figure back to me I could tell by her warm smile that she was quite pleased.

I saw a shape coming toward me in the murky darkness. "Don't be alarmed. It's José."

I greeted him, and he sat down near the mosquito netting. We talked for quite some time. I told him what a joy it was to be around Zoila and him and to bask in the warmth of their relationship. "Your relationship is so simpatico," I said, noting an orange twinkle of a star just above the dark outline of his head.

"I think this is because of me," he said. "I've always been easygoing. Zoila is more moody than I am." There was a silence, and then he laughed lightly.

"Why did you fall in love with her?" I asked, hoping my question was not too pointed.

He answered quickly and seemed happy to talk in detail about their marriage. "We have always had a deep physical attraction. But it was not simply sex. We both have a great and enduring love for the earth and for her life within us. That is what we have always shared." He paused and said, "Everyone grows differently. No two flowers are the same, but they can grow in the same garden. When I see a flower, I see the sun and the light from Zoila's body, and it's all the same. The flower is her life and her spirit, and it is mine also. Simple, no?"

"No," I said, laughing. "It's a blessing."

José wished me a good sleep and disappeared into the night. I heard the door to the house open, and then I heard the three of them laughing and talking. I petted the yellow dog and thanked him for leading me to the goddess figure. In a few minutes we were both asleep.

I awoke at dawn to the crowing of the cock. The old yellow dog was lying flat on his back against me, his four legs sticking straight up. His extended muzzle was snuffling and wheezing with an occasional snore. I rubbed his tummy. He rolled over, not venturing to open his eyes. I jumped to my feet, rolled up my bedding, and took down the mosquito netting. I left the dog lying there contentedly and went into the house. José and Agnes were at the table, and Zoila was frying tortillas and eggs. I saw that a plate was set for me, and I joined them.

"Help yourself to some fruit," José said. "Breakfast will be ready in a minute."

I selected a mango, cut it in half, and began eating. After breakfast I did some housework, and then Zoila called to me to follow her. We went into the small room with the table altar.

"This altar was made by my grandfather and given to me by my grandmother," she said. "It does not have a nail in it. When I received this altar I did a ceremony behind a curtain and then came out carrying it by a sash tied around my neck. I cured a lady of asthma and was told that I had the power to make the face of the earth stand up. An altar, a mask is like a spirit. It is lazy and sleeping. You have to learn to make it stand up. You have to sing like this."

Zoila, amidst the crowing of the rooster and the barking of the yellow dog who wanted inside, began singing. The words, of course, were Mayan and therefore not intelligible to me. She conveyed that she was a young girl who was lost. Then her song became almost coaxing, as if she were trying to entice the spirits. She was certainly enticing me. I could feel the walls and the floors become alert, if that is possible. Every once in a while she would intersperse her Mayan with English words. "I want your beautiful elbows and arms, your strong hands, your mouth," as if she were singing to a lover. I could feel a response within myself as well as within the room. Agnes tiptoed in and sat in the corner with her pipe held in the crook of her left arm.

Presently Zoila began laying out her bundles and explaining each to me. This took at least two hours. From time to time I would glance at Agnes. I saw that her eyes were closed as if she had fallen asleep or gone into a trance. I had never seen her show respect for another medicine woman in quite this way. I felt privileged to share Zoila's extraordinary knowledge. She explained many teachings that I had previously not understood, stressing the new responsibility I incurred by receiving this knowledge. It was dusk when she put away her bundles.

Next we began working with my few bundles. I floated over her altar, her face of the earth for several hours, as if entranced. The construction of her altar was different from either the first or the second one she had drawn for me yesterday in the hut.

She explained, "I use different altars for different purposes. World altars for instance, are for ceremonies to help the world. These

ceremonies are usually held up on the mountains or on the
volcanoes. The sun marks the place where you situate the altar and
the sun tells you where to feed it. It is in a different place each day.
Each time the sun comes up, different deities carry it. Where the
sun comes up or goes down, that is where you feed your mask of the
earth and every position walk has a name. All mountain altars have a
tree, and some trees have three altars of stone. One faces directly
toward the equinox and the other two face solstices. For these altars
you gather thirteen deities or powers."

"What kind of altar are we working on?"

"This is a divination or personal altar. In the mountains or outside
we use stone. In the house we use wood like this table. Inside this,"
she said, tapping the wooden top, "the altar carries items
symbolizing all things personal, personal deities, and time deities,
and their positions. Also color, animals, mammals, flyers, swimmers,
reptiles, and herbs are all part of the personality of your altar. The
power of the south corner is my dream and my vision. It is how I
establish my friendship with a particular ceremony. Sometimes there
is hail, or the white falcon, or a leaf cape, but there is not body or
form, for it is made of solid wind. Inside there is an open plain,
where I present offerings."

A glowing white light shone around Zoila, and I believed that she
was in a trance. Her words had not all made sense to me and had
not all followed one another coherently. I had seen Agnes in a
similar state several times, but this was the first time I had seen
Zoila this way. Her explanation was so beautiful that the feeling
emanating from her words made it all sensible to me.

There was a long silence as Zoila seemed to be looking into
another world. She continued, "Before you do anything, after you
have situated your altar properly, you station your guards, soldiers, or
mountains at the four corners. This is so nothing bad can get in.
Then you take your incense, copal, and your 'main man,' the
hermaphrodite, and set up the peace providers and the warriors.
Women are the strongest warriors. Set obsidian blades there by
them at the four corners. They help. Then kiss, blow, set up incense
with your hand. It's like rain. Making rain is sexual. For the very old

and very young there is no rain. Remember your 'main man' is
made powerful by what is around him. Everything else follows. The
woman-man is delicate like the heart and sits on a chair or throne
toward the top center of the altar. To the right of her-him, you
place your court of female deities on hollowed-out stone thrones.
These deities drink from these stones. It is to these deities and the
hermaphrodite that you give your first wrapped bundles. These are
bundle offerings. They are like babies, beautiful offerings; bundles
are like seeds. Make the outer shells beautiful, then unwrap them to
expose the germ, the seed or placenta of food or water inside. Open
them and offer them to the deities, blow on them, and set them in
front of the thrones. They are my court to other worlds."

I noted during each phase of her endeavors how lovingly she
performed the acts. She put candles along the upper angle of the
altar and carefully lit them all. Then she painstakingly put out
tobacco, sugar, flowers, cigars, and incense for each deity. Then she
placed all the bundles in the center plain and opened most of them.
We discussed the need for positive and negative influences. Zoila
seemed to dwell on this point because the balance of positive and
negative items creates power. Lastly she placed a wrapped bundle in
the right-hand corner.

"No one ever sees what's in that bundle, not even José," she said.
"That is my medicine animal, known only to me. She is my great
ally. Strength is what is going on here." She swept her hand over
the altar. "Pray for a word, for contact with your own personal star.
You will learn to animate your altar, your mask of the earth with
power and make her stand up."

Zoila went over my bundles with me and showed me how to
place them on the altar according to dark and light, female and
male.

"This is a representation of every part of my sacredness, my
psyche, my mental being, and my physical being, isn't it?" I asked.

"Yes, it is. The altar enables La Sabia to take out of herself what
is intangible and place it tangibly in a sacred position with the sun,
moon, and stars so that she can work with it to heal herself and
others. The altar enables you to take power out of the mind and

place it in the hands of the deities of the earth and sky."

"Do you use your altar often for divination?"

"Yes," Zoila answered, "when I want to be scientific and make no mistakes. One can use different methods to divine the probable, but not the future."

"Which way do you use to divine the probable?"

"We call it lightning blood or twitching. It is the most powerful. When lightning hits its mark, it shivers. When you twitch you know that it is good."

"That makes sense to me. When you used your sun stone on my shoulder, I felt a twitching sensation from your hands. Is that what you mean?"

"Yes. I will speak of the typical way I work. In our own village, when someone comes to me for healing, say a lady who has trouble in her womb, the woman talks to my people first and brings a gift of food for my in-laws. It makes them soft. If a shamaness eats the food too, she cannot refuse the patient."

"Then what happens?"

"Later the woman will come back with an entourage and sit. The entourage is to witness and see if I'm a good shamaness, and they help the patient remember if necessary. We talk for a while until she finally says what she thinks is wrong. Then I ask for one half-pint cane liquor, three cigars, three white candles, and white copal, and they get it for me and bring it to me in a cloth wrapped like a baby. I accept it and lay it on my altar just as though it were an infant on her back, and I open it so the deities can recognize the offering. The deities sit on mats. Ajpop is the lord of the mat, and I give big *ach* prayer offerings that carry words, and I put these words in my smoke like rockets as an introduction to the name. If there is no name, you can't be recognized. There is no face."

"What usually happens?"

"I heal her, and everyone goes home."

"Are different incenses used for different ceremonies?"

"First of all, each incense has a deity. We use white copal for the mountain altars, for the biggest world ceremonies. Copal is resin from the copal tree here in the Yucatán. Ponto copal you use and leave inside. Bark copal is best for getting rid of enemies and fear. You can add salt and chili to incense for cleaning yourself or a house."

I stood silent for several minutes. Agnes had joined us and stood on my left. We both surveyed the altar, covered now with dozens of pieces of crystal from various shamans or power spots, pieces of bone, stones of every color and shape and size, strands of hair, fur, cloth, perfume, a crucifix, images of different saints, tobacco, flowers, herbs of every possible description, silk scarves, weavings, paper cutouts, arrows, feathers, prayer sticks, precious stones, and many unidentifiable objects.

"It is a beautiful and sacred sight," Agnes said.

I nodded my head in wondering approval.

We said prayers together. Agnes held her pipe over the face of the earth and we prayed in our different languages to the Great Spirit, who was able to understand all. We prayed for health and continued life on this great Mother Earth.

That evening Agnes and I drove back to the hacienda and slept for a good twelve hours.

Mirrors are glass, sad glass! In our Mother's belly
I tumbled with a twin, looked in her eyes.
In the old time what we know was dangerous to know
when others tumble around this world so lonely, so lonely.

Philip Daughtry

# Chapter 11
# The Sacred Twins

At noon I went over to have lunch with Zoila. I was really hungry, and I wolfed down my food. Zoila ate slowly.

"I see you like your tortillas," Zoila said.

I couldn't answer because my mouth was stuffed, but I nodded that I did.

Zoila took a small bite of fruit. "My grandmother taught me that there are many mouths of which we are unaware."

"What are they?" I asked, after swallowing my mouthful.

"Mouths of people and animals are the obvious ones. But less obvious are the mouths of trees and spirits. Everything alive has a big mouth, or else it would be unable to exist. Have you ever come across a living entity without a mouth?"

I thought about it. "No," I said.

"Everything surviving birth is hunting for food to fill its mouth."

I laughed.

"Your body itself is a big mouth. It needs all kinds of nourishment to stay fed—air, water, beans and rice, sunshine, love, understanding, among others. Inside your body are other universes, all of which need to eat. One very important mouth is the one that lives between the two rounds of intention that you call your conscious mind and your unconscious mind. This mouth, like any other mouth, needs food. In the world of shamanism, finding the proper food is everything. Finding the proper food for, say, a spirit,

will keep it alive. If it's a bad spirit, you'll want to find and take
away its proper food, so it will soon move on. This is very
elementary, but it is a crucial point."

I had actually stopped eating. "Can you define food for me,
Zoila? What exactly do you mean?"

"I mean substance, that which supports a life form. It could be a
carrot in some cases. Or food could be good or bad thoughts,
language, or truth. In other words, energy in any form needed."

"Can you give me an example?"

"Think of Agnes for a minute. You've seen her turn into another
life form right in front of you, such as a grizzly bear."

"Yes."

"Haven't you ever wondered how she does that?"

"I think I know."

"It's not exactly a commonplace occurrence. How do you think
she takes on these animal forms?"

"Well, she must focus intently on becoming what she wishes to
become, such as a grizzly bear."

"Do you believe she actually becomes a grizzly bear?"

"I don't know. All I know is that she has developed the power of
intense focus."

"Focus? Don't you see you're not saying anything of substance?
What you say is true, but how do I use that?"

I didn't reply.

"Agnes does this very difficult task by bringing forth a harvest of
totality. Think of that and all that it implies. By totality, I mean
Agnes understands attention and being. When this happens, we see
marvels. Life is something like a motion picture. Everything you see
is a thought form. Imagine that a form is a circle that is held
together by sound. For that is exactly what a thought form is.
When you learn the sound of a form, then you have discovered a
part of its diet, its food. Why do shamans go around chanting all
the time and making weird noises?"

"I don't know. Why?"

"Those sounds are part of a form. If you want to disappear,
become invisible, take the sound out of a thought form and poof! If

you want to seduce a spirit and make it yours, one of the things you do is sing to it. Words, sounds, tones, they are all part of what holds our reality together. Never is there a life form without sound. Agnes thinks "bear" with her total attention and doesn't remove 'bear' from her being, and she is a bear. When you think "bear" you may see the image of a bear in your mind's eye, but it is very flimsy."

"How do I make my thoughts take the form I want, so that I can manifest them?"

"Agnes first sees a bear in her mind, just as you do. Then she shifts that vision to her solar plexus and lets it become her total attention. She finds the sound that is the food for its mouth, and puts its form together with her total being. She wills it into being by the very fact that she can will you to see it."

"Now I am confused. What do you mean, she wills me to see it?"

"She knows your food too. She sees your spirit mouth and feeds it. She knows what songs you need to be able to see and she knows that she exists only because you agree to it. You agree for her to change into the image of a bear, and that bear is real."

"You mean it's a real bear, and at the same time it's a trick?"

"It's a trick only insofar as everything you see is a trick similar to the trick of a motion picture."

"Agnes has often told me that what we see is like a reflection."

Zoila placed her hand on my arm.

"Let's take, for example, the mouth between your two minds," she said. "Everything has a mouth. This universe has a mouth. The mind is a universe, and each of your two minds has a mouth. Do you agree that what you call your unconscious mind is a storehouse for all the knowledge you possess?"

"I agree."

"Do you agree that your conscious mind is a great life tool, and that it has little access to your unconscious and all its great wisdom?"

"I suppose."

"There is much confusion about how the mind works. Are you aware that all of us are both male and female?"

"Well, Western psychologists have theories about the animus or male and the anima or female sides of the personality."

"This is difficult for me to explain in English, but between what
we would call the islands of your conscious and your unconscious is
a great mouth. Your unconscious mind eats almost everything. Your
conscious mind eats only what it needs to stay stable and rational.
These mouths both eat the process of translation."

"Translation?"

"Yes, translation of the language of one island into the language
of the other island. Two runners or messengers travel between the
islands. They are the only ones who can come in and go out of the
mouth. To all others, the mouth is closed. The messengers are called
your sacred twins. They, and only they, are the translators. They
fight like warrior and warrioress for the balance of your
consciousness.

"I still don't know what you mean by the word *translation.*"

"It's a fact that if you have the wisdom of all the ancient peoples
of Mother Earth stored on your island of the unconscious you will
never know it, because it is simply nowhere on your island of the
conscious. Therefore it will remain unknown to you. It is to your
sacred twins that this duty and responsibility falls. They will bring it
from one island to the other."

"How?"

"Since ancient times this has been accomplished by dreams and
visions. Why does Agnes tell you to fast and go on vision quests? It
is because she knows that for the sacred twins to be able to reach
you and each other, and translate messages, all blocks to this process
have to be eliminated. Dreams and visions are the essence of
sacredness. You must be still to smooth the path for your sacred
twins."

"Many psychologists do incredible work in the area of dream
interpretation."

"This is very difficult. And it is further complicated when you
interpret someone else's dream or vision."

"Why is that?"

"Because dreams are private. We are imperfect beings seeking
perfection. We do not see clearly. So how can we interpret dreams

clearly, especially if the dreams are inventions of someone else? The messages are cryptic and scrambled and therefore difficult to understand. In many cases we can only guess."

"That doesn't sound promising." I said.

"That's why you must make direct contact with your sacred twins. They can bring messages directly from the island of the unconscious. They can speak to you in a clear language you can understand. You don't have to interpret anything."

My eyes lit up. "Are you in direct contact with your sacred twins?"

"I am."

"How do I meet mine?"

"Maybe I can lure them out for you. But first, you must ask me to teach you."

"Zoila, please teach me. Please try to introduce me to my sacred twins."

"Good," Zoila said. "To teach you, I must first be asked. I will do my best."

We finished eating. I had lost interest in my food and ate only mechanically. We cleared the table of gourds, bowls, and leftover food. Sunlight flooded the kitchen as we did the dishes. No children were at Zoila's or in the entire village of Llano, for that matter. Everyone had gone to the next village to see a puppet show put on by one of the schools there. It was very quiet without them.

When we had finished cleaning the kitchen, Zoila said, "Come."

We entered the small room with two windows. I noticed a small hole in the dirt floor in the middle of the room that I hadn't noticed before. Near the east wall sat her rectangular table altar. On it were different things than the other day or they were arranged differently. There were candles, tiny colored jars of flowers, a gourd dipper, wrapped bundles, some small clay pots, an old book that was yellowed and falling apart, a snakeskin, and a variety of other items I didn't recognize.

Zoila lit the candles. She saw me looking at the table and said, "Remember, this is my house altar. I use it rarely. I like to use my stone altars outside under the cieba trees for most of my work. This one is more personal, and very few have seen it. It's my foundation altar.

She unrolled a grass mat and placed it on the dirt floor with one end under the altar table. "There," she said. "Please lie on this mat with your head here under this point of the table while I prepare our way."

I adjusted my clothing, and got comfortable, feeling a little foolish looking up from underneath at the wood of the altar.

"You can go to sleep if you like," Zoila said. "It may take a while."

Copal smoke began to fill the room. I was tired but not sleepy. Zoila began to sing and talk in a sing-song fashion in Mayan. I closed my eyes and listened, relaxing my body and my mind, which seemed to be generating nonsensical thoughts. My thoughts were interrupted when I felt cool drops on my forehead and arms. The liquid was sweet smelling and minty. I opened my eyes as Zoila knelt and placed a few yellow and white flowers on my chest. I smiled, thinking that I must look like a corpse.

"Get up," Zoila said. "You've been sleeping."

"No, I haven't," I quickly replied. "My mind was just wandering."

"Well, get up anyway. We have to go on a journey."

"Where to?" I asked. My voice was impatient. "I didn't know we had to go anywhere."

"Give me the flowers," Zoila said.

Sitting up, I handed them to her. She put them in a clay vase on her altar.

"Wait. You'd better smell them before you go."

I leaned over and smelled the blossoms. I was irritated because they didn't have a perfumed scent, good or bad. They just smelled like weeds.

"Let's go," Zoila said. "You have an important date, and I wouldn't want to miss it."

"Date? What kind of date?"

"Open the door, and let's go. I'll follow you."

"Door. I don't remember a door being here. All I remember is an adobe mud brick wall."

"Open it," she insisted.

The door was old, old wood, hand-hewn, and hung on rusty iron hinges. It squeaked loudly when I pushed it open. I walked out onto the path a few yards.

"I'm right behind you," Zoila said. "Keep going."

I felt her breathing behind me.

I had trudged along for maybe ten minutes when Zoila said, "Oh, no."

I whirled around. "What's the matter, Zoila?"

"Don't be alarmed. I just lost my eyeballs. It happens all the time. Do you see them anywhere?"

Aghast, I searched the ground but didn't see any eyeballs. I was starting to get frightened.

"Lynn, it's OK. I'm sure I can find them later. Do you mind if I hold onto your arm? You can guide me. After all, I wouldn't want you to break an important date." She grabbed hold of my arm just above the elbow.

"Are you sure you're OK?" I asked.

"You just follow the path, Lynn, and I'm sure everything will be fine. Don't get lost, though. If there's anything I can't stand, it's being lost."

"I won't," I assured her.

But I was wrong. I was totally disoriented. I didn't recognize anything. We were in rolling hills with *chimisa* and scrub brush in every direction.

"I don't remember any of this from before."

"Any of what?" Zoila asked. "Remember, I've lost my eyes."

"We seem to be in a desert, Zoila. This doesn't look like the Yucatán. This looks like a place I know near Palm Springs, California."

"Oh, I wouldn't worry about it," Zoila said. "You're probably just seeing the jungle from a different perspective."

"If you say so," I said. I kept on the path, Zoila still holding onto my arm. I don't know what I would have done without her comforting presence. I was very insecure and wanted to cry, but I was ashamed to do so. At least I had my eyes. I tried to concentrate. I didn't see the sun anywhere. It would have helped me

get my bearings. Instead, what I saw was a kind of naked twilight, I
had no idea where the light was coming from. I was in a place
unlike any place I had ever been before.

As if the situation weren't bad enough already, with the lost
leading the blind, my own eyes started playing tricks on me. The
plants started looking like animals. I thought I saw a sagebrush jump
from one place to another, appearing to be a bobcat. I thought the
plants had animal spirits. But when I looked at them closely, they
became plants again just to irritate me.

"Zoila, you won't believe this, but I think the plants are animals."

"Why do you say that?"

"Well, one of them has a snout. I think they're trying to fool me.
They jump around, but when I look at them they stand stock still. I
don't know how much of this I can take."

"If I had just one eye . . . but I don't. If you say the plants are
animals, I have no alternative but to believe you."

"Which way now, Zoila?" I asked, feeling uncomfortable. "This is
making me nervous," I said as Zoila adjusted her grip on my arm. I
was completely bewildered.

"Don't forget to guide me," Zoila said. "I may trip and fall." She
gave me a nudge.

In front of me was nothing but sand. It had a queer iridescent
glare. We walked across the sand, and the land became a hard clay
plateau. It was parched and broken open in countless thirsty cracks.
I described the terrain to Zoila, and she said she thought we were
exactly on course. What course? I wondered.

I saw something bobbing up and down, and realized it was a man
coming toward us. I was appalled, because it might not look right
for two women to be out here alone, and one of us was blind.

"Zoila, there's a man coming toward us. Do you know that?"

"I'm not surprised," Zoila said, "considering the way things have
been going. What's he doing?" Her voice sounded like she was
talking into a jar.

"Still coming. No, wait a minute. He's stopped. It looks like he's
waiting for us. He looks kind of menacing."

"Keep walking until you get close enough to speak to him."

As I got closer I saw that the man was an Indian. He appeared
very sturdy, a feisty fellow not unlike Geronimo. His arms were
crossed, and, from the look in his eyes, I felt he was challenging me.
A few feet from him, I stopped.

"Describe him to me," Zoila said. "Is he Indian?"

"Yes."

"Where is he from?"

I asked him, and he told me.

"He says he's from the mesa, wherever that is, and that he's
Apache."

"What's his name?"

"What's your name?"

"Oh, you can just call me Sam," he said. "You wouldn't be able
to pronounce my name. Now who were you just talking to?"

"Why, I'm talking to Zoila, of course."

"Who? I don't see anyone."

"Zoila, he says he doesn't see you. He must be blind as a mole."

"Play along with him," Zoila said. "Pretend it's a practical joke.
I'm invisible to him and also inaudible. You have to tell me
everything. I'm really sorry I lost my eyes. I'm getting a little deaf,
too. I wonder if I'm going to lose all my faculties."

"Who are you talking to?" the man asked gruffly.

"Oh, no one," I said. "I talk to myself. It's a habit I got into
when I was little."

"I don't like to be made a fool," the Apache man said. "Don't lie
to me."

"I promise. I'm not talking to anyone but myself."

"That's telling him," Zoila said, squeezing my arm. She told me
to repeat everything the Apache man said. I did so.

"What kind of expression does he have?" Zoila asked. "Is he
happy to be here?"

"He doesn't look like it. He looks angry."

"Ask him why he's angry?"

"Are you mad or something?" I asked.

"He's upset because it's taken so long for me to reach him," I
repeated to Zoila. "He says he has much to tell me, but I'm always

unaware. I rarely remember the dreams he sends. What's he talking about, Zoila?"

"Don't worry about it. Describe him to me in detail."

"Well, he's about six feet tall, about my age. No, he says he's younger, but I don't think so. He seems a bit argumentative. He wears long black braids, high leather moccasins, pants, and some kind of loincloth over them. He has a rifle slung over one shoulder and a bow and quiver of arrows over the other. A sheath knife hangs from his beaded belt. He has red paint and many scars on his face, but his eyes are kind. He's beginning to laugh at me."

"Do you like him? Do you think you can be friends?" Zoila asked.

"I like him a lot."

"Why do you like him?"

"Because he is obviously a dedicated warrior. I think that's the predominant reason. The warrior's path is an art to him. He's stealthy and smart. He says he's so much like an animal that he wears paint on his face to make himself appear human." Zoila and I both laughed out loud.

"Does he like you, respect you?" Zoila asked.

"He says that I'm all right. I think perhaps he does."

"What does he think about your life up until now?" Zoila asked.

After listening to his response, I answered Zoila. "He feels that I have accomplished some tasks that have provided me some satisfaction. He says that I don't enjoy myself enough or have enough fun, though. I'm in need of less work and more time to experience play. He says that play is an important aspect of the warrior's demeanor."

"Is he glad that you've come here to meet him?"

"He says that he was about to give up and go back on the warpath. He says that he wants to be my ally, but he will be an adversary if that's what's needed."

Zoila chuckled, but I felt it was a gibe coming from the Apache man. He walked slowly to me, extended his hand to my heart, and said, "It was almost too late for us." He removed his hand and put it in the same place over his heart.

I told Zoila what he had done and asked her what he had meant by it.

"He's expressing how happy he is," Zoila said. "Ask him what you can give him."

The question absolutely delighted Sam.

"I don't have one with me," I told Zoila. "He wants a new macaw power feather, red with a pointy end."

"I have one of those right here," Zoila said. I turned and took the feather from her. "I have lots of them," she said. "Give it to him."

Sam took the feather from me and seemed very pleased. He touched it to his forehead and then put it in his quiver with his arrows.

"Zoila, he wants to give me something in return."

"What is it?"

"Skunk fur!"

"Ask him why he wants to give you skunk fur."

"He says it will keep away my enemies."

"You'd better take it, Lynn."

I took the fur he offered and put it in my dress pocket. Sam seemed rigid and formal, and his eyes stayed on me intently.

"Ask Sam if he will translate for you."

"Translate what?"

"Just ask him, and tell me what he says."

"He says he will bring gifts and guidance from one lodge to the other. What's he talking about?"

"Never mind!" Zoila snapped. "Ask him how best you can hear him when you are in a normal state of consciousness."

I had the urge to tell Zoila she was acting rude and making too many demands on me. After all, I had my own mind and the ability to make decisions as to what I should ask. But everything was so strange, I didn't raise the question. Only a few hours ago I was— where was I? Oh well, it didn't matter.

"What did you say, Zoila?"

"I said to ask him how best you can hear him when you are in a normal state."

I asked.

"He says that if I will sit down with a pen and paper at night before sleeping, that he will come and help me write. I don't want him coming to my house, Zoila. People think I'm weird enough already."

"We'll sneak him in," Zoila said. "No one will know."

"Well, in that case it will probably be all right. He'll have to sleep in the guest bedroom, though."

"I'm sure he won't mind where he sleeps. Thank him for his gift and offer to help. Tell him that we're going to continue on our journey, but that we'll be back, and we'll see him later."

"He says he will wait for us no matter how long it takes."

"Good," Zoila said. "Let's see now. Keep following the path we are on. We'd better hurry. We might miss her." With that, she shoved me firmly.

I hurried on, still leading Zoila. She seemed in such a hurry to get there, somewhere or another, that I walked along as fast as I could. The desert had a blue and green sand surface that seemed to be glowing. The path was clear, but I couldn't see any footprints. It seemed peculiar. We were now in a valley, and we began to walk over and around massive boulders. Then it struck me that the rocks were jewels—emeralds, diamonds, rubies, sapphires, and garnets. I could hardly believe it. They were more beautiful than ordinary jewels, and they were several stories high. We came to a place where the path forked, and I asked Zoila how best to proceed.

"Go left," she said.

"Have you ever been here before, Zoila?"

"Not here, but I know a place exactly like it just like the back of my hand."

Her explanation satisfied me. The surface of the land was now pure white, a little too dazzling, and it appeared as though we were climbing slightly, gaining elevation. It was unlike anything I had ever seen—much whiter than snow. I accepted this completely astonishing landscape as a matter of course. Then I started to hear music, music unlike any I'd ever heard. Choirs were singing, and a thunder clap would occasionally interrupt. It was beautiful but didn't seem to fit the occasion.

"Zoila, you're not going to believe this."

"What?" Zoila asked.

"There is a ballerina dancing up ahead. She's so good that she's spellbinding."

"Go to her," Zoila ordered. "And remember that she can't see or hear me. So you will have to tell me everything that happens and everything that is said."

I promised I would and excitedly approached the dancer. She was up on her toes spinning. She stopped when she saw me coming. She was tall and slender and looked as though she had just stepped off the stage of the Bolshoi. Her hair was up on her head, and she wore a king's ransom in jewels. She had magnificent long, tapering fingers.

We greeted each other, and I asked her many questions. Her answers were very sophisticated.

"Tell me what she says," Zoila asked.

"Her name is Lala and she is a Russian prima ballerina. She is very beautiful and accomplished. She told me her whole life story, practically. Would you like to hear it?"

"Never mind for now. How old is she?"

"She's older than me, about forty-five I guess."

"What does she think about your life?"

"She says she thinks I have chosen a very interesting way to express myself. Not many people are willing to share magic. She says the ballet and movement are two things that I would do well to know more about. She also says that if you take care of your body, you are never too old to dance. She seems pleased with me, though."

"Is she happy to meet you?"

"Oh, yes. She says she is delighted. She says she has wanted to meet me for a long while, and she wants to meet again soon. I wonder if she would come to Los Angeles and stay with me for a little while?"

"Ask her when she will visit you."

"She gave the same answer as Sam. She says that every night just before sleep she will come to me. I'm going to have a house full of company. I don't know where I can put her if Sam has the guest room."

"Ask her if she wants to give you anything," Zoila interrupted.

"Don't you think that would be kind of rude, Zoila? I've only just met her."

"Customs are different here. That's the way things are done."

"I didn't realize that."

I quickly asked Lala what, if anything, she wanted to give me. She gracefully walked a few paces and picked up something shining. She brought it to me.

"Why these are really splendid, Lala. Thank you so much. Zoila, she has given me a pair of gold earrings."

"Give her something in return. Give her your ring."

With some hesitation, I slid the opal ring off my finger and gave it to Lala. She immediately put it on her finger. It was dwarfed by her other jewels.

"I'll treasure it," she said.

"Now ask her if she will accompany us back to meet Sam," Zoila said.

I asked, and Lala agreed.

We all set off, Zoila clutching my arm and Lala dancing happily around us, back through the valley of the jewel boulders, until we came to the fork in the road. It was an area of weird delights. We were all laughing like a bunch of schoolgirls. I didn't have much desire to see Sam again so soon after we had left him, but I could tell it was important to Zoila. When we finally reached him, he was sitting cross-legged on the sand. He watched our approach with sharp eyes. About ten paces in front of him, we stopped.

"Sam," I said, "We've brought you some more company." Lala stopped pirouetting and seemed a little perplexed by Sam's appearance. "Sam, I'd like you to meet Lala."

"What's going on now?" Zoila asked.

"Beauty and the beast are meeting for the first time. Sam is getting up and standing straight as a board. Lala looks polite but put off. I think she's shocked at what Sam is wearing. He doesn't seem to like her tutu either."

"What's Sam doing now?"

"He's crossed his arms and stuck his nose proudly in the air. He's grunting at Lala. She's asking him if he can speak. He says he'll speak if she'll change her ridiculous clothes."

"What does she say?"

"She's looking at him murderously. Wait—now she's laughing and telling him that he's quite right. She's starting to spin, faster and faster. It's making me dizzy. She's coming to a stop, and now she's wearing a long red satin gown. She looks very aristocratic. Sam is nodding his head approvingly."

"Do you think they can be friends?"

"I think so, but they are obviously quite different. I think it may take some time. Lala says she will enjoy trying to change his bad habits. He says he doesn't have any bad habits. She says that he is apparently quite uncivilized but more appealing as a friend than many of the fops that she knows. He may be too harsh to spend much time with, however. Sam is saying she looks like someone who danced out of a department store window, and that he dislikes women who are smarter than him. She's humoring him."

"Can you get them to embrace each other?"

"No. Lala says she won't embrace Sam until he takes a bath. He is saying that he likes only Sacred Sweats and that it's none of her concern anyway."

"We have accomplished much. It's time to return. Thank them for meeting you, and tell them that for now, you will look for them before sleep every night. Even if they drop in for just a moment."

I told them, and they seemed sad that I was leaving.

"We understand," Lala said.

"Thank you for the macaw feather," Sam said.

"And thank you for the ring," Lala added.

"Goodbye," I told them. I was a little sad myself.

Zoila said, "Do you mind if we go back a different way? I know a shortcut."

"I don't mind."

"Good," she said, "Hang on."

She tugged at my arm, pulling down on me. Suddenly we were going up, not down. We were going backward at an incredible rate of speed, like a film does when the images move in reverse. I went in through the door backward and found myself smelling the flowers.

"How did we get through that door backward?" I asked.

"What door?"

"Why, that door right there."

"I don't see any door. You must be imagining things."

I examined the mud bricks, pushing on them. Zoila stood near me, amused.

"Well, it was right here. I swear it. What did you do with it, Zoila?"

"Perhaps it is closed for now," Zoila said.

I jerked around. "You remember, don't you Zoila?"

"Of course I remember. But now is not the time to speak of it. You'd better take a few deep breaths. You look pale."

I breathed quickly and deeply several times. I was trembling all over. My stomach felt hot, and I was quite dizzy. I felt Zoila's hand reach around my waist to support me. She led me into the kitchen and ducked my head in a bucket of water. It revived me for the moment.

Zoila threw me a towel. I dried my hair and started to get up and make some tea.

"Not yet, Lynn. Stay out of your habits. Stay totally in the physical world."

Zoila insisted that I work for several hours. She gave me a small hand ax and told me to chop a huge pile of firewood into kindling. When I finished chopping, I stalked the teapot, but she scolded me and told me to continue working. She gave me a long list of things to do: wash windows, wash clothes, pick fruits and vegetables, hoe weeds, clean the house. It would have taken me two days to finish.

I had a tendency to drift off into daydreams. Each time I did so, Zoila yelled at me angrily. She seemed to catch me each time. Once she actually shoved me into the wall near where I was standing with a wet sponge, swiping at windows that were already perfectly clean. I was so shocked that I grumbled out loud about my treatment. Zoila shoved me again.

"Let yourself be angry!" she insisted.

That took the sting right out of the barb. How could I let myself be angry when she gave me permission? I couldn't get angry at all, and, as I thought about it, I had to laugh.

Zoila cursed me in several different languages, upbraiding me for being stupid and lazy. "You think you're too good to clean my house!" she said. "You're condescending and you're pretending like you're working only because you want something from me."

I was hurt by her words. I flew into a slow rage and threw the sponge at her. She jumped out of the way, and I missed her. I threw the sponge so hard, that I pulled a muscle in my shoulder. I started after her, but before I could catch her she vanished. I walked around the house howling in frustration, wanting blood. Then I started crying.

As I sat in the garden drying my tears, Zoila reappeared. "Now we can enjoy tea together."

She had brought a tray, and she set it down on the bench next to me.

"I'm sorry, Zoila," I said. "Can you forgive me for losing my temper?"

"Forgive you? I worked hard to get you that mad. I had to get you back *here*, and right now. It is very important. I've seen people who have experienced what you have, who haven't come back for a year. But I think you're all right now."

"I feel like I'm mostly here," I said. "You know, I find it hard to believe what just happened. By the way, what did happen?"

"You met your sacred twins."

"Sam and Lala?"

"Yes. To take you there I had to use an old Mayan trick. Of course, you didn't go anywhere except inside yourself."

"None of that was real?"

"It was all completely real."

"Did you go with me?"

"Not exactly. I stood beside you while you smelled the flowers. That was my reality. I tricked you into thinking I went with you. That's why I told you I was blind and deaf, so you would explain everything to me. I acted as a sort of guide. Even though I was not with you, I do know the territory. It is nearly the same for everyone.

But in order for me to go with you, I would have had to shift and enter into the same consciousness with you."

"Are you saying that everything that happened to me was totally in my mind?"

"Yes, of course. What happens to you always happens in your mind."

"But wasn't it real?"

"Absolutely."

"Were Sam and Lala real?"

"Yes, completely real."

"And you say you could have come with me and had experiences that would have been just as real for you?"

"Yes, I could have. But I preferred to stay in this ordinary world rather than go with you."

The whole thing was puzzling. I didn't know what to believe. How could there be two realities when reality, by its own definition, is that which is real? I scratched my head and realized my opal ring was missing.

"Did I give my opal ring to Lala?" I asked.

"You did."

"What happened? How did you experience that?"

"The ring disappeared off your finger, that's all. You never budged from smelling the flowers. That was my experience."

The conversation was an eerie one. Whenever I found myself in these strange worlds, the experiences were unquestionably real. It seemed as if only then did my experience of the world come alive; all other experiences seemed shallow. But Zoila said I was also standing in her altar room, smelling the flowers. Were the sacred twins real or not? Was it all a dream? And how had Zoila managed it?

"Enough lessons for today," Zoila said, cutting off any further inquiries. "Come inside."

I followed her. In the kitchen she handed me the gold earrings and a piece of skunk fur. "Don't lose these, Lynn."

I looked at her in amazement.

What is this joy? That no animal
falters, but knows what it must do?
That the snake has no blemish,
that the rabbit inspects his strange surroundings
in white star-silence? The llama
rests in dignity, the armadillo
has some intention to pursue in the palm-forest.
Those who were sacred have remained so,
holiness does not dissolve, it is a presence
of bronze, only the sight that saw it
faltered and turned from it.
An old joy returns in holy presence.

Denise Levertov
"Come into Animal Presence"

# Chapter 12
# The Jaguar Mask

The next morning after silently doing my various tasks, and a reflective breakfast during which neither Agnes nor I spoke, I finally discussed some of my troubling thoughts and tried to frame them into logical constructs.

"Agnes," I said, "my mind is boggled with everything that has happened here. I still find it difficult to believe we are here together. And yet here we sit."

"You've said many times that you believe the saying that truth is stranger than fiction," Agnes said, a merry twinkle in her deep brown eyes. "You're right."

"I'm glad to hear you agree with me for once," I said, joking. "When did you arrive at such a conclusion?"

"I watched television while I was waiting for you the other day."

"What television?"

Agnes pointed. "Over there and down that hall. They have a dish that picks up satellites. The program was called "Star Trek." Did you know there was a man from another planet who has strange pointy ears?"

I stared at her. "You watched that?"

"I did."

"Agnes, you amaze me," I said.

She winked knowingly over her mug of hot milk and strong coffee. "Yes, that program was wonderful, and it was interesting that the writers foresee a military design for our future voyages into space. I certainly believe that too, but I have a different concept of martial intent. I found the story to be very entertaining. You would certainly have to be a brave warrior to stand before creatures with omnipotent powers."

"Sort of like yours," I said. "Right?"

Agnes frowned.

"Well, Agnes," I said, "I'm in no mood for anything unusual today. I don't think I could metabolize one more ceremony or anything else out of the ordinary. I would lose my mind." Agnes's face seemed to darken, but I went on. "So what do you think about shopping in Llano? Maybe I could buy you a new blouse."

"Nope."

"What do you mean, nope?"

"I mean nope. I want to watch more teeeveee." She stretched out the word.

"Television? You? You must be kidding. Maybe we could have lunch together like civilized folks."

"Nope."

"Just nope?"

Agnes shook her head.

"OK, I'll see you later then."

"Have an ordinary day."

Oh, well, I thought to myself. Agnes probably needs a day of rest and a break from me. I excused myself and left the hacienda.

I drove my rented car into the village. I felt like driving, because every muscle and bone in my body was exhausted. I simply wanted to play tourist, sip a lemonade, and look at curios. I parked the car under a tree in the shade. I locked the doors and strolled across a narrow dirt street to get my drink. I went inside the door of a restaurant that had outdoor tables clustered around a fountain. Standing at the counter, I fumbled in my purse for some pesos and paid the owner for my drink.

I strolled around the village, sauntering along, looking into store windows at odd moments. I went into a shop that had some colorful blouses and dresses on display. Eye-level racks held shawls and brightly colored embroidered dresses. I put down my lemonade for a moment to look at the shawls. I didn't find anything I thought Agnes would like. When I reached for my drink, it was gone. I swore under my breath. I looked around, wondering if someone had taken it. The storekeeper saw me searching around and said in broken English, "Amigo. Outside." He pointed to the door.

"What friend?"

"Amigo. Outside."

I went out to look. There, sitting on a bench and sipping my lemonade, was my old friend Drum. He got up and stood looking at me with a wide grin on his face.

"What in the world are you doing here?" I asked.

He greeted me with open arms, and we both sat down on the bench. He handed back my lemonade.

"Nice of you to return something that doesn't belong to you," I said. I took a sip, noticing that the contents were half-drained.

Drum seemed to be in an enthusiastic mood. He was wearing new blue jeans, brightly polished cowboy boots, and a beaded belt buckle. A Bull Durham tie hung from the breast pocket of his western shirt. His eyes were veiled beneath a wide-brimmed Stetson hat. He was tricky looking. I was more than a little nervous about how easily he had sneaked up on me and stolen my lemonade.

My mind went back over my history with this young Cree Indian man. When I first met him, he was Red Dog's number one apprentice. So much had happened since then! I had taken the stolen marriage basket back from Red Dog, causing him untold anguish and a loss of power. Drum, along with Red Dog's other apprentice, Ben, were told to leave. They had become Ruby Plenty Chiefs's apprentices. We had all become tentative friends over the past few years, but I hadn't seen either of them for some time.

"Why are you here?" I asked.

"If you'll buy me lunch, I'll tell you."

"Let's go," I said.

We set off at a leisurely pace down the street, passing a couple of shops. Finding a small restaurant that served local specialities, we went in. We sat at a red plastic table that was set with white paper napkins. A large propeller fan twirled overhead.

After we had ordered and were chewing on chips and salsa, I said "How are you? Are you and Ben still with Ruby? What's the matter, Drum? You look preoccupied."

"Wouldn't you be?"

"I don't know. Are you having problems?"

"I hitchhiked all the way down here from Canada. Did you know Ruby kicked us both out?"

"What happened? I hadn't heard anything about it."

"She said we didn't have enough discipline. She told us to go join the Army."

"You and Ben are pretty lazy, Drum. You probably *don't* have enough discipline—self-discipline, anyway."

"Maybe. I don't know. But hell, we weren't apprentices, you'll have to agree. We were a couple of slaves to that old witch. She was damned near meaner than Red Dog. I'm glad she kicked us out. She never once talked to me or Ben that she didn't tell us something else we had done wrong. Good riddance!"

"I see you didn't join the Army, unless you're AWOL."

"Hell, no! They make everybody the same. We went searching for another teacher. First we went to Phoebe."

"Phoebe!" Phoebe was a demented woman who had taught Red Dog paper magic and witchcraft.

"Phoebe said in her weird way to go ask Red Dog first. I think they ought to put that woman in the nut bin. She said Red Dog had come here to the Yucatán with twelve new powerful apprentices."

"Here?" I groaned, pretending not to be aware of his presence in the vicinity.

"Yeah. And guess who he's discovered is around?"

"Who?"

"Why you, of course." Drum's eyes were menacing for a moment.

"Why me? I'm a nobody!" I exclaimed. "It seems like a man as powerful as Red Dog would have better things to do with his time."

"No one has ever rivaled him for power the way you have. You defeated him. These sorcerers don't look at things like a normal person does. He has an old score to settle with you. You know that. Don't act so damned innocent. You reclaimed the marriage basket, and he'll never rest until he evens up the score."

"Well, believe it or not, I'm just down here on a vacation."

"Lynn, cut the crap," he snapped between bites. I noticed the salsa was dribbling down his chin. "I'm no fool. I can smell the power lurking around here. To tell you the truth, I've found Red Dog."

I became guarded. "Oh, really," I said, as nonchalantly as I could manage.

"Yeah. He said I would have to prove myself to him. He said he didn't trust me anymore, and maybe even Ruby sent me down here to spy on him. He started treating me like he was some kind of damned drill instructor, like I was a lowly recruit. You can't fight him. He's always in control, and he just took me over. He gets inside of you, and you don't have any choice but to obey him. This time, though, he's on a real power trip."

"Red Dog sounds just the same to me, Drum."

"I learned a lot from Ruby about my female side. You might not believe me, but I don't want to go back and serve the great Red Dog. I think he's evil. All I want, all I ever wanted, is to become a big medicine man, not a sorcerer. I learned a lot of rules and such, but that sorcery stuff's spooky. Half the time Red Dog had my britches scared off. I need your help, Lynn. Please."

"What is it you want me to do, Drum?"

Unexpectedly, he reached over and placed his pouch of (Bull Durham) tobacco in my hand. His face was sincere.

"Find me a teacher, one I can respect and one who won't treat me like a slave."

"I can't guarantee that. But I suppose I'm obligated to do what I can," I said, nodding at the pouch of tobacco, which I had placed on the table next to my plate.

That was Drum's cue to start shoveling in the beans. He ate ravenously, and I wondered if he had missed a few meals.

"What ever happened to Ben?" I asked. "Did he come down here with you?"

"No, we split up in Wyoming. He said he wasn't going to let Red Dog use his brain for a playground. He wanted to try something new. He was going to see that shaman named David Carson."

"David Carson. We've talked about him before. Where is he located now?"

"Somewhere in the southeast part of Oklahoma, a little place called Tuskahoma."

"Isn't that where the Trail of Tears ended?"

"Yes, I think so. For the Chactaw tribe, anyway. Ben thinks this Carson is going to take him on as an apprentice and teach him how to kick Red Dog's ass, which seems to be his life's purpose at the moment. He's still pretty mad at Red Dog for dumping him, and he thinks this Carson is the answer."

"What do you think?"

"Well, I've heard some pretty weird stories about this Carson's powers. They give me the holy terrors. I'm not going to fool around with him myself."

"Well, I wish Ben the best."

We ate the rest of our meal in silence, even though Drum's mouth was moving like a freight train burning coal.

When we were finished, I said, "Come with me, Drum."

I paid, and we got in my car and drove over to Zoila's.

"You better wait here in the car, Drum."

"Yeah, I know how it goes. I'm prepared for the worst."

"Don't be so optimistic."

I went up to the front door and knocked. José let me in and searched my face as he led me into the main room.

"Could I speak with you and Zoila, José?"

"Zoila isn't here."

We talked. I gave him the tobacco that Drum had given me. Then I gave him a brief summary of Drum's history. Finally, I asked him if he would meet with him now and consider taking him on as an apprentice.

"Was this Drum's tobacco?" he asked.

"Yes, he gave it to me and asked me to lead him to a teacher."

José held the pouch to his heart and closed his eyes.

"Yes," he said, more to himself than to me. "I will meet with him back at the restaurant you were just at in half an hour." He smiled at me. I had the uneasy feeling he knew something I didn't know.

"Thank you, José."

"Thanks are irrelevant," he said.

I left and went back out to the car.

"You're on, Drum. José will meet with you at that same restaurant in half an hour. He's a special man. Shall I drive you there?"

"No, I'd rather walk," he said, getting out of the car. He started walking off in the direction of the village, then turned back to me. "Grassy ass, Lynn!"

His joking way of saying "gracias" did not amuse me. He walked off down the road. I turned the car around and headed straight for the hacienda. I couldn't wait to tell Agnes about my encounter with Drum. There went my quiet, ordinary day. I was feeling uneasy. Despite Drum's show of great sincerity, I felt that something might be wrong.

The sky was screening over with dark clouds, and rain was threatening when I pulled up and parked in the hacienda driveway. I ran up to the room. No one was there. It was deserted. The oddest sensation came over me. It must have had something to do with—I didn't know what. And Agnes had mysteriously disappeared.

The room was perfectly tidy. My canvas hanger bags were hung neatly in the closet. I sat down for a moment and tried to center myself. An eagle feather lay on my pillow. I took it and studied it. Agnes had often told me that an eagle feather had the power to guide a person in time of doubt. Something was really wrong. I knew that now. I stared at the feather for so long that it began to blur.

The thought came to me that I should go to the hut in the jungle at once. I tried to remember exactly where it was located, but my memory failed me. I had been so many places in the jungle! My mind traveled over the dirt road, and I remembered the fork we had taken. I picked up my goddess figure, my sun stone. I put on a shawl in case of rain and shut the door quietly behind me as I left.

I set the eagle feather on the dashboard. After taking one wrong turn, I found the right road. I heard a crack of thunder, and rain began to fall softly. I parked at the edge of the jungle, locked the car, and ran down the path through the rain. The verdant tangle of vines and creepers were an obstacle. I kept wrapping my shawl around me, and it kept coming loose. The trail was so narrow that I had to stop many times to get my bearings.

Finally I came to the field where the hut was located. Smoke was pouring from the chimney, and rain was still falling. Terror hit me once more. I was more certain than ever that something terrible had happened. Frantically, I ran toward the hut. A huge dog sprang out of nowhere and blocked my path. It was the yellow dog, but now he seemed dangerous. He growled as I approached. He arched his neck as though he were going to leap. I remembered the goddess figure, the sun stone. I took it out of my pocket and showed it to him. He growled. My heart was hammering. I inched closer, holding out the figure. He snarled even more menacingly. Fortunately, he sniffed the stone. It worked like a password. He started to whine and wag his tail. He licked my fingers and let me pass. I thanked him and patted his head with a new respect. The dog followed me inside the hut, and I shut the door behind us.

The room was gray with smoke. Rows of women were sitting on the floor, and some women were standing. I recognized a few of them, even through the dimness, as women who were staying at the hacienda. About thirty were congregated here in this one place. I could hear the patter of rain now as it came down faster. Lightning flashed, and a quick explosion of thunder rattled the hut. In that instant I realized two things: One, this was some sort of convocation, and two, I was in the presence of the Sisterhood of the Shields. I sat down in my tracks between two women.

I saw Agnes standing in the front of the room with Zoila and the woman I had known as Jaguar Woman. Seeing the three of them filled me with an odd mixture of emotions—awe, love, tenderness, and a feeling of belonging. Jaguar Woman moved forward out of the shadows. She was not wearing her white stone jaguar mask now. Instead her face was painted with black and red diagonal stripes across her nose. She seemed so familiar and yet so different at the same time.

"What has happened?" I quietly asked the woman on my right, but she was as puzzled as I.

The room lapsed into a silence punctuated only by the sound of the rain beating on the roof. The three women were now sitting on mats facing the rest of us. Then Zoila rose.

"The jaguar mask has been stolen," she said.

For several moments a commotion raged. Then the women settled down, and the noise died away. The copal smoke was so thick it made the faces of various women pass in and out of the smoke puffs like ghost faces in a dream. Some kind of unknown energy surged through me. I felt an intense pressure on my ears, and I seemed to leave my physical body for just an instant and float above it. I heard myself saying, "Do you know who stole the mask?" My voice sounded far away.

"Red Dog stole it, with the help of his twelve apprentices."

"Are you certain?"

"He has made it known."

Jaguar Woman stood. "Come, Lynn," she said. "Sit down on this mat closest to me."

I glided between the women, found the mat, and sat down near her. Jaguar Woman was leaning slightly forward. She stared at me without emotion.

"To steal a shaman's mask," she said, "is to steal her face, her way of praying and doing ceremony, her life." Her eyes burned into mine. "You have learned recently about the altar, the face of the earth, the mask—and you have discovered how to unite with power. You have been initiated into the mysteries and the way of the shamaness. One day you too will receive your face, your own power mask, and you will understand what it means.

"The jaguar mask predates the Sisterhood of the Shields and even the pyramids. With the jaguar mask in the hands of an evil sorcerer, it could do untold harm. It could even spell the end of the sisterhood. It is the principal face of the sisterhood and it must be reclaimed."

A light began to shine in the room. I was not sure how this had

happened and wondered if my mind was playing tricks on me.
Perhaps I was projecting into external reality what I felt within
myself. I was bolt upright and felt a warmth deep within me. A
drum was placed in my hands, and I leaned back and began to beat
it. I was astonishingly good and seemed to drum the heartbeat of us
all. Voices blended in a chant. Zoila sang in old Mayan. The song
built in power, like a whirling dervish and ended abruptly. The
curious light was abnormally bright, and I sensed a great anger
among the women.

"You have been told to use your anger in a constructive way and
not let it turn into fear," Jaguar Woman said, looking closely at me.

All at once the yellow dog began to growl and pace back and
forth in front of the door. I saw a flash of white teeth. He made
weird, unearthly sounds. He shivered in anticipation and then
barked several times, sniffing along the bottom of the door.

"Quiet him," Jaguar Woman said. "Keep him in."

Several women began petting him. He finally became docile and
sprawled in front of the door. Everyone returned to their mats, and
our attention returned once more to the front of the room.

"You helped the sisterhood once," Jaguar Woman said.
"Unknowingly, you will help us again."

I blushed and became self-conscious. I tried unsuccessfully to
overcome this and remain calm. My throat began to constrict, and
this exasperated me. Jaguar Woman came forward. She knelt in
front of me and held out her left hand for me to see. I stared at a
large butterfly cocoon nestled in her palm. She took the cocoon in
her right hand, which was painted red. She shook it, and something
fell out into my left hand. Someone began playing a lilting song on
a clay flute.

"This is a gift from your sisters to fortify the power that you are
still unaware of having."

"Thank you," I said. "All of you." I indicated the other women.

"You are the youngest here," Jaguar Woman said. "Your
innocence has brought us life once again, just as a butterfly is born
from a cocoon."

The object in my hand was tiny, but heavy for its size. Agnes

brought a lit candle and held it close to me. Now I saw that I held
a gold goddess figure with butterfly wings edged in black obsidian.

"It's beautiful," I said. "Thank you again."

"Thanks are not necessary. Understanding is. You hold
Itzpopolotl, the obsidian butterfly goddess. She is the goddess of the
hunt. She is head of the obsidian cult of the magical weapon. She is
also a goddess of death. Long ago in our history, she also became a
Mayan goddess of the melon cactus and a goddess of the abundance
of the earth. Obsidian is related to corn and the production of food,
but it also is a relative of death, night, and the sacrifice of the heart.
The heart sacrifice was always performed with an obsidian blade.
This is the dark side of the obsidian butterfly. She is our guardian
and will bring death and destruction to anyone who steals the face
of the sisterhood."

I peered down at the gift. I imagined what ancient wonders and
horrors this goddess must have witnessed.

"How shall I help you?" I asked.

"Tonight you will begin to understand at the jungle temple of the
jaguar. The sisterhood will hold a ceremony to raise power for the
hunt. Wear Itzpopolotl in a cocoon pouch around your neck. You
will need her. We will take power mushrooms so that we can see
this intruder who would destroy us. Prepare. Do not speak or eat.
We will gather when the moon is high." Jaguar Woman receded
into the shadows. Agnes indicated that it was time for us to leave.

Agnes and I went through the jungle and directly to my car.
Minutes later we were sweeping down the rutted jungle road toward
the hacienda. I thought about what had just happened. I was
uncertain and afraid. This gathering of the sisterhood had reminded
me of my deepest dreams in that it was incomprehensible to me. It
was as if I had been carried there on powerful yet invisible strings. I
wanted to question Agnes, but I had been ordered by Jaguar
Woman not to speak. My heart swelled; the dignified power and
strength of those women was almost more than I could bear.

Bizarre images kept creeping into my mind, images of a blood
sacrifice on a stone altar. I saw an obsidian knife plunge into Red
Dog's chest. I shuddered. It wasn't that he didn't deserve it, but if

he died, who would be my good enemy? What was I thinking of? I tried to clear my head of my demented thoughts. I shifted to glance at Agnes. Her face was inscrutable and darker than the night forming outside. I fingered Itzpopolotl through her cocoon.

Inside our room at the hacienda, Agnes sat on the bed, her hawk-like face staring at the shadowy walls. We said nothing. We ate nothing. Around eleven o'clock we got in the car and drove through the back roads in the jungle. I tried to relax as I drove but found it impossible. My apprehension was mounting. We drove for more than an hour.

Agnes leaned toward me and whispered, "Park."

This was it.

I was glad Agnes knew where we were, for I certainly didn't. We walked down a path lit only by the moon shining through the vines and the towering trees. I had never been so deep into the jungle. The night sounds were intense. Cicadas and birds screeched, and my throat was dryer than ever. I was near terror, wondering what fate awaited me.

The heavy perfume of night-blooming jasmine filled the air. Agnes's dim shape moved silently ahead of me through the moonlight. I could not hear my footsteps on the path, but I could imagine them in my head. A vine slapped me hard in the face. "Ouch!" I cried to myself, feeling a nasty welt. I reached up and ripped it away.

I was more careful now not to collide with the sea of vegetation. I was paying strict attention. Still, I wondered what I was getting myself into this time. The trail curved abruptly. Agnes hesitated for a moment and looked up. I followed her example. There in front of us was a huge unexcavated temple covered with ferns, and vines and ringed about by swaying trees. The edifice was yellowish-brown and thrust upward hundreds of feet into the sky. It looked like the fist of a giant reaching up out of the earth to snatch the moon away. Then the drums sounded, very slowly, with a beat every five seconds or so.

Agnes continued on. I followed her around to the left of the temple. I kept glancing up as we hiked near the outside boundaries. I soon realized that the temple had been excavated on one side but not the other. We came to a bridge built of great stones, where two Amazonian women blocked our way. I thought I recognized them from the ceremony of La Ultima Madre. Each wore Mayan masks composed of shiny gold metal that appeared very thin and pliable.

"We are here to guard the masks," one of them whispered to us. She held out a strange-looking plumed mask to Agnes, who quickly put it on.

I was also handed a mask. I didn't have time to examine it, because it was thrust into my hands and I was made to understand that I should put it on immediately. I did so. In the darkness all I could feel were long thin feathers running down the back, slits for eyes, and an open mouth. My hand slid over a countoured relief of snakes that bordered the crown. Part of the mask was metal, and part was cloth. Because of its dark color, I felt as though I faded into the shadows. The shapely feathers settled on my neck and back.

I followed Agnes past the two guardians and over a stone-surfaced terrace. She motioned for me to come alongside her. She whispered in my ear, "Find Jaguar Woman and do as she says."

Before I could say anything, she vanished around the corner of a high stone wall. I didn't know what to do, so I followed her. Rounding the corner, I came to a perfectly excavated grassy quadrangle slightly smaller than a football field. On all four sides, stepped pyramids loomed up several hundred feet into the night sky. Flaming torches had been casually placed around the perimeter.

Mayan trumpets or *hoptas* droned from somewhere, and the drums began to beat at a quicker tempo. Once in a while a trilling flute could be heard, and a string instrument would purr and carry into the winds of the humid night. As the music played, I crossed under an arch in the stone wall and went around to the front of the main pyramid. What I saw made me gasp. Hundreds of candles zigzagged up the steps and around the quadrangle, lighting up the night. They looked like a mammoth jeweled fire snake winding over the earth and stone.

Waiting on the other side of the quadrangle was a throng of masked women who had formed into a crescent line in front of the great pyramid. Most wore simple white dresses embellished with

ornaments. All the masks and headdresses were different—a
bewildering array—some ornate and typically Mayan and some
simple in design and color.

I joined the line and did what the other women did. We moved
subtly to the music from time to time while gazing up at the
hieroglyphs and carvings near the crest of the pyramid. It was as
though I had slipped out through a secret door and had wandered
into a celebration on another planet.

The music began to play faster, and I was beginning to forget
myself completely when suddenly there came a crash of cymbals, a
bleating of *hoptas* and flutes, and a licking flash of flames from a
fire pit at the top of the temple. Many masked women carrying
small torches filed down both sides of the temple steps. The
warrioress masks adorning these women were grotesque and
nightmarish, with a certain malicious beauty. The masks glimmered
in the firelight, and the moon shone directly above us.

The women formed into a single line, their high plumes
shimmering in the firelight. I sensed that these women made up the
Sisterhood of the Shields.

Jaguar Woman appeared on the temple steps, and the whole
quadrangle became silent. Wearing jaguar robes, she held up her
hands, or paws—even from the distance where I was standing I
could make out the sharp claws. She was holding an intricately
carved staff in her left hand. Her face was again painted black and
red, and the absence of the mask was painful to witness. But even
without the jaguar mask, she conveyed a remarkable feline splendor.
I felt the ancient tuggings of a tradition as old as time, a tradition
that was part of my heritage as a woman on this earth.

Seeing Jaguar Woman caused my heart to flood with an
overwhelming emotion. I saw much of my own life. I was born a
woman, and because of this I was shunted aside, consigned to the
hollows and fringes of life, where so very many of my sisters
continue to reside. Was it simply historical accident? I tried to see
through the mirage of social barriers that cloud the eyes of women
the world over. We don't even recognize each other. It is as if for
centuries we have moved like chromosomal mutations isolated from

the gene pools of the originally sacred, our primal female nature
stolen from us, from the world pool, just as though it never existed.

I stood gazing at the silver layers of copal smoke that filled the
air. It smoldered up from swinging tureens held by several of the
women. A drumbeat sounded. It pounded through the jungle night
in unison with the rushing of blood in my ears. The lines of masked
women began to sway. Then the persistent drumming quickened.
We chanted and sang and danced in and out of the trailing copal
smoke that wisped up and formed a giant serpentine cloud. The
lines continued to move. Each of us blended into the colorful
throng. We were enraptured, as if the drumming were the totality
and we were a part of the sound. On and on went the drumming,
and then it ceased abruptly.

An explosion of orange light belched from the fire pit. We looked
up and saw that Jaguar Woman was pointing across the quadrangle,
where thirteen dark male figures holding thirteen burning torches
stood in a line at the top of the opposing pyramid. Even through
the smokey air I could tell that Red Dog was among them. I felt
faint. I recalled the extraordinary vision I had once had. Years ago,
in this vision, I had mated with Red Dog as the Kokopelli, an
irresistible Indian doll-like figure, on an altar in a place just like this.
An icy chill moved up my spine. The vision had not only balanced
my male nature and my female nature, but it had been my first
recognition and acceptance of my own dark side. Perhaps it had
been a premonition of this very night.

I clutched the butterfly goddess through the cocoon around my
neck and tried to banish my thoughts of Red Dog's heart being
ripped out by an obsidian blade and then being lifted up and offered
to the sun. The images were unbearable.

Red Dog was wearing the jaguar mask, and he threw his head
back regally. His apprentices all had haughty swaggers and were
scantily clad.

"So you dare to come here wearing my face! Speak your name!"
Jaguar Woman called to Red Dog over our heads in a surprisingly
soft tone. Her voice carried perfectly across the quadrangle.

"West Woman, hear me," Red Dog said loudly. "You ask for

names. Names are unimportant. I am a man of power, and I come
here from the north."

"Why have you come here?"

He spoke menacingly. "I have come to take your power. I have
come for your good death and to steal your dreams. I will assume
the power of your face."

"You are wearing it," Jaguar Woman said. "Assume its power."

"I intend to," he said. "But this toy means nothing to me
without the keys of knowledge that you hold that will unlock its
power."

My legs felt rooted in the earth as I watched this exchange
between the sorcerer and Jaguar Woman. The jaguar mask that Red
Dog wore sat atop his muscular body and gleamed like an insidious
mirror in the glassy moonlight.

"Then return the face," Jaguar Woman ordered. "It is of no use
to you."

"No!" Red Dog shouted angrily. "Mine!"

"Then why should I teach you, a bandit, a thief in the night?"

"Because I had the power to take it, and you are weak." He
waved his bare arm threateningly. "You are not worthy of such
power. All of you are unworthy. You should stop your foolishness
and go home."

The silver copal smoke briefly obscured Red Dog from my sight. I
was cringing and saw in the semidarkness that the women who stood
near me were also frightened.

"Man-from-the-North!" Jaguar Woman called. "What you say is
true. You have terrible powers, and you have done an awesome
thing. On this very night we will take mushrooms together if you
are willing. If you are a coward, of course, you do not deserve
power. I will teach you some things about the Jaguar mask, and you
will see that it has even more power than you have imagined.
Perhaps within the sacred dream we can find the answers we are
both looking for. Is that acceptable?"

"Don't you realize that I am a man, and I am not a coward?"
Red Dog said in a strange voice. "You will see that I am worthy of
power. I agree to this test. It is acceptable."

"Then descend the pyramids, and we will meet in the quadrangle."

With Red Dog in the lead, the men came forward down the steps. The Sisterhood of the Shields also began moving toward the center of the quadrangle. The line of women had begun to edge away from the procession when Jaguar Woman walked directly to me and handed me a large, deep bowl with the image of a turtle on the bottom. It was, I knew, called the eagle's bowl.

"Take this eagle's bowl, and follow me," Jaguar Woman said. "Watch what happens carefully. You are the Water Woman tonight. Take no mushrooms."

I clutched the bowl to my stomach. I knew it was an ancient blood bowl still vibrating with the beating hearts of thousands of sacrificed victims from ages past. I stepped into line behind the sisterhood, and we all followed Jaguar Woman. A sparse drumming and a trilling of flutes had begun. I was afraid for the very existence of the sisterhood. How could this body of spiritual women take mushrooms together with a proclaimed sorcerer and his dreadful apprentices? I was horrified to think what that might lead to. How very odd that Jaguar Woman would even suggest taking this food of the gods with avowed enemies. I had also heard magic mushrooms referred to as flesh of the gods. Agnes had told me that many of the ancient Mayan ceremonies and healing rituals had involved the use of power plants and mushrooms, but she had never used them in teaching me. I wondered what the consequences were going to be and I began to have an inkling that something fantastic was about to happen.

More shrill flutes and mandolin strings joined the music, and it crescended into a mountain Peruvian style of song. I could see some female musicians up on the pyramid steps standing in a row. While playing they rocked back and forth in time with the beat and melody. We had come to the center of the quadrangle. We stopped. A lone cieba tree stood there, and Jaguar Woman stood and waited in front of it as Red Dog advanced on her. His apprentices were fanned out on either side of him like a Plains Indian raiding party preparing to attack. These men wore full body paint of various designs. Their faces were artfully painted, and traditional feathers were tied into their long hair.

Red Dog seemed to have gained an enormous amount of power since I had last seen him. He drew up to Jaguar Woman, walking proud and tall. I respected him in many ways. Though the moonlight was obscured by clouds and the torches were held high, it appeared as if he had regained the original red of his hair. It had been gray for the past few years. His lean body seemed to hold a compressed energy, like that of coiled springs. The stolen jaguar mask peered down on us all. His apprentices were also lean, muscular, and aggressive looking. Some wore leather leggings, but most of them wore just a loincloth and leather beaded moccasins. They did not speak or smile or turn their heads.

The apprentices had stopped several yards away, but Red Dog was so close he agitated me. The mask transformed him in some imponderable way into a monstrous being. On Jaguar Woman the mask had appeared almost male. On Red Dog, however, it was female, evilly female, as if it were hiding a Death Mother waiting patiently to devour us all.

Jaguar Woman said in a husky voice, "Bring the mushrooms, and set them on mats between us."

Two women moved around in front of us. They unrolled mats and set out several bowls of mushrooms and a tureen of water. They lit candles and burned copal incense. This was a cue for many of the sisters to come forward and place offering bundles on the mats. This was a give-away to the spirit of the mushrooms for a good journey.

A stiff wind rustled my hair. Then suddenly all the women were chanting, led by Jaguar Woman. The female musicians moved down the pyramid steps and through the quadrangle toward us. I could see their forms silhouetted against eddies of light from the burning candles. The wind gusted again, and a thick blanket of copal smoke enveloped us. The music expanded into a frenzy, then stopped suddenly.

A silence ensued, in which the standing men regarded us with open hostility. Jaguar Woman indicated for me to bring her the first

mushrooms. I did so, nervously approaching the mats and returning
with several of them in my blood bowl. Jaguar Woman took the first
mushrooms and began chewing. A few light strums on the strings of
some unknown instrument followed, and very faintly the flutes
began to accompany it.

Then thirteen women, including Jaguar Woman, moved up to sit
in a line touching the mats, not more than a dozen feet from Red
Dog. Jaguar Woman motioned for Red Dog and his apprentices to
be seated across from them on the other side of the mats, which
they did. Mushrooms were passed down each of the lines of women
and men. Each person took several and ate them. Jaguar Woman
was sitting directly across from Red Dog and, as far as I could tell
when I passed the water in the blood bowl or when I was sitting
down in the rear of the group, she never took her eyes from him
nor did the other women look away from the gaze of the men
opposite them. Every so often a man's head would droop and he
would appear to be sleeping, and then he would raise his head back
up. The women seemed to be in perfect control.

About twenty minutes of silence passed. Then Jaguar Woman
said two prayers. I saw several of the men's heads fall forward, then
jerk back to attentiveness.

Red Dog whispered, "Discipline!"

Jaguar Woman began to chant in a most exotic, liquid tone, "I
am mother of the Clown Woman. I am the Jaguar Mother." She
repeated the second line several times.

A woman blew out the candles, and the men's torches were
extinguished. The men and women appeared to be blue
phosphorescent forms in the moonlight while she chanted.

> Use the darkness as a background
> for your seeing eyes.
> You will not need light to see
> the keys before you.
> The wise ones are with us.
> We see them clearly.
> They wish to tell you.
> They wish to tell you.

She repeated these lines several times and added several variations. The chant lasted for quite some time with more variations of the former chants. I had never seen a ceremony such as this, so I had no idea what to expect. The chanting had an unusual vibration and seemed to sweep back and forth in time, echoing into the gloom, being born and reborn when the accompanying music would reach a heightened pitch. The chant was so forceful that at some moments it would terrify me and at other moments it would lull me into a hypnotic state.

Red Dog and his men were definitely under its spell. They listened and watched giddily—their attention was total. Their painted bodies glistened in the firelight. One man with half-open eyes reached out an arm toward the woman opposite him. The woman remained perfectly still. I was uneasy, but the man finally dropped his arm.

Jaguar Woman's voice became delicate and took on a warm, seductive tone. Her silhouette swayed in tempo to the music. I could see the other women in fingers of yellow moonlight. They were kneeling, their bodies heaving like waves, rolling voluptuously. Each of them moved supplely, just as though they were very graceful and very young women.

> See the beauty before you.
> See the beauty before you.
> I am the Hummingbird Woman, ho!
> I lead you to food, ho!
> The Eagle Lord waits in the trees.
> He sees your skeleton.
> He sees your blood burn.
> See the beauty before you.
> Burn.
> See the beauty before you.
> Burn.
> I want your legs.
> I want your beautiful knees.
> Hummingbird Woman prays.
> I want your arms.

I want your toes and fingers.
Prays.
All power within us now.
All power within us now.

One of the males hissed through his teeth. Another motioned
imperatively for the woman across from him to come to him. This
was no ceremony at all. I didn't know exactly what was happening. I
wanted to tear off my mask and rub my eyes. Three of the men
were standing, swaying erotically on their well-muscled legs. Red
Dog himself stood. One man held out his arms to the woman across
from him, beckoning.

The music had a warm, velvety quality. The air was thick with
sexual tension and copal smoke. I felt I was participating in a
sacrilege; everything was moving toward the forbidden. I could
hardly bear to sit still. Some of the women were swooning between
chants. Jaguar Woman's voice was now husky and even frightening,
like nothing I have ever heard. She trilled like a nightingale between
phrases. The tone of her chant surged like waves falling on the
ocean shore.

I took it all in silently, but I was trembling, taken over by the
seductive sounds of the night. I tried to comprehend the surprising
turn of events. I had an almost irresistible urge to run away, but I
didn't. All the men were standing now. Red Dog actually leapt
over the mats and embraced Jaguar Woman. He drew Jaguar
Woman to him, crushing her to his chest. I saw their bodies as one,
fire-bathed in the torchlight. Animal sounds emanated from Red
Dog's throat.

The other male apprentices followed a like scenario with the
women. Bodies were stripped naked, and everyone danced, swooning
and falling on the grass; it was as if all previously hidden impulses
had been unleashed. I closed my eyes and chanted, thinking that I
had truly taken leave of my senses. As I was struggling with my
exploding intellect, I felt something cold and round being shoved
into my hands. I looked down. I began to tremble, because I held
the Jaguar Mask.

"Guard this," Agnes whispered in my ear.

I was afraid to move away from the group, for I wondered if someone might see me carrying the mask away. I tried to fit it in the blood bowl, but that didn't work. I waved frantically for Agnes, but she had disappeared. I crawled around on all fours trying to find a place to hide the mask. Finally I settled on stashing it under my blouse, holding it firmly to my stomach.

I sat up, tried to look as inconspicuous as possible, and watched motionlessly. I wondered how long I was going to have to endure my plight. I won't try to describe the carnal exhibition I saw of entangled and writhing bodies.

"Lynn," I heard someone say from behind me.

I turned around. Jaguar Woman stood with the other women. What a surprise!

I jerked my head around back toward the naked bodies. It appeared as though the men were with young women, but these female forms began to dissolve, leaving nothing in their place. Now the men were moaning ecstatically and very definitely enjoying themselves alone.

"What did I just see?" I asked.

"You saw projections of desires," Jaguar Woman said. "You saw men enamored of their own delusions."

When I looked back at the men, I saw half-dissolved images in the arms of the men. The images faded in and out of focus.

I felt a hand grab my arm. It was Agnes.

"Come now," she ordered.

I got in line with some other women. As the entire procession of the Sisterhood of the Shields filed out of the quadrangle, we chanted:

> You are clean now.
> The wise ones say.
> The eagle says.
> You are clean now.
> We are well-trained spirit women.
> I am the Jaguar Woman.
> Pray.

You have been torn from the mountain.
The spirits pray.
The spirits pray.

Before I left, I had the urge to take a last look at Red Dog and
his apprentices. They were naked in the moonlight and the red-gold
torchlight. They were moving eagerly, rhythmically, merging their
souls with deception. The musicians stayed behind and were still
playing. I surpressed an urge to laugh out loud.

In the hacienda the sisterhood gathered in a large room. It was
before dawn, and a few candles were lit. I could hear the wind
outside whispering softly; it made the candles flicker. I still clutched
the jaguar mask to my naked skin and it filled me up. I gazed
intently at these beautiful sisters, for I had the feeling that I would
soon be leaving the forests of the Yucatán.

A circle was formed, and Jaguar Woman called me to the center.
The shadows of the women played across the white adobe walls in
fantastic shapes, like disowned parts of my own being.

"Do you have the mask?" Jaguar Woman asked.

"Yes," I said.

Pulling it out from underneath my blouse, I presented it to her. I
thought I saw the glimmer of tears on her face in the weak light. I
moved back to the circle. The shadows again stirred in shapes—
amorphous cutouts animated in some indescribable way by the same
spirit that was within me. I watched my own shadow merging with
others and then pulling away.

Jaguar Woman held up the mask for all to see. It was like an egg
floating above us or like the moon. She went around the circle,
beginning with Agnes, and each woman touched it a moment. I felt
honored to have been able to carry it even for a few hours. I was
the last to place my hands on the jaguar mask. I saw it now as a
radiant, shining globe bestowing protection. A strange blue light
crept up my arm, and my entire being felt whole. I took my hands
away hesitantly and felt a twinge of sadness.

Jaguar Woman placed the mask over her face slowly, turning so
all could see. A great joy and exhilaration was felt around the circle.

"The face has been returned," Jaguar Woman said. "The great sisterhood is ever restored and recreated."

There was tremendous excitement. A light, a vast glowing, began to manifest itself from these women. I wondered if my eyes had been too civilized, if I was now seeing something I should have always been able to see. Then the glow lost power and dimmed.

"Stand in the center," Jaguar Woman said.

Again I moved to the center of the woman circle. Jaguar Woman joined the others. Everyone, including her, removed their masks and set them on the floor, so that there was now a ring of faces gazing up at me from an odd angle. The room grew dark. The faces on the floor seemed to hold an ominous power. One woman began to sing a plaintive song. She was joined by clay flutes, which blended perfectly with her soprano. The lyrics were in a language unknown to me.

All the women began moving closer to me, pushing their masks with their feet as they inched nearer in a sluggish dance. The masks crept closer, the music grew stronger, and the women seemed to take on animal shapes. The masks were egglike luminous disks, that lifted, or so it seemed, upward. I experienced an implosion of energy and a state of merging into oneness with the universe.

The next thing I knew, I was sitting on the floor, still in the center of the circle. The masks were halfway between me and the women, who were also seated on the floor. I now saw their painted faces in a vague light.

"That was a song of gratitude," said Jaguar Woman in her deep voice. "Now you must receive your face. You have returned the face of a medicine woman, and that is a great act. You have lent power to the sisterhood. You must understand what you have done."

"But Jaguar Woman, I have done nothing."

"Quiet, child," she ordered. "I will try to explain." She paused without smiling and then said in a firm voice, "Out of darkness, intolerance, prejudice, and imbalance, you are working to reveal the power and sacredness in all women. You, and many others of our sex, are beginning to remember who they are. You do not yet remember completely who you are, but soon you will know."

"How do I lend power to the sisterhood?"

"Do you remember that when we met previously in the hut, the yellow dog, the guardian, began to growl and want to go outside?"

I was bewildered. "Yes, I remember."

"He was growling at an intruder who was spying on us."

"Who? Why didn't you let the dog out to catch this spy?"

"Because I wanted him to hear us."

"Why?"

"Because otherwise Red Dog would never have found us at the pyramids and the mask that had fallen into his hands would have remained there."

"I don't understand."

"You brought Drum right to us. He followed you."

"Drum?"

"Yes, he never met with José. It was a trick."

"Why would Drum do that?"

"He had to prove himself to Red Dog before Red Dog would take him back as an apprentice. Is that not correct?"

"Yes, but how did you know?"

"José sent word immediately."

"Did Drum lead Red Dog to the jaguar pyramid?" I asked.

"Yes, and it was good. He fell victim to his own evil web. Bring light to your weavings, or don't sit at the loom. He and his apprentices have all been taught a lesson they well deserve. They've fallen into their own inevitable mirage and they won't quickly recover."

I heard giggling, and I looked around the circle. Spirits were so high that I felt compelled to laugh myself.

"You thought you were witnessing an orgy, didn't you?" Jaguar Woman asked.

"Well, yes. I thought I was, I guess."

"Nothing happened except in their minds."

"But I thought I saw you. Was it like a hologram?"

"Listen to me. When the spirit of the mushroom enters within a shamaness's body, she can take any form without. She can make an old man young and handsome, a warrior. She can call in the flying shields or make an old woman such as myself appear young and seductively beautiful. When those men looked at us they saw what they wanted to see. They were seduced by their own lust. We lent our vision to their vision and conjured up images that would hang them. The curious thing is that a black sorcerer is always seduced by his own vision of greed and fear. The only way to make a sorcerer change his ways is for him to begin to see that power will eventually turn on those who misuse it. When those men awake from their sensual reverie and discover their folly, there is no way that they can avoid the truth."

"It certainly looked like you made love to them."

"To conjure for the uninitiated is simple. To conjure for the trained sorcerer is an entirely different thing. They are not taken in so easily. Yes, it appeared as if we made love to those men. Never come into an enemy's territory and use her weapons without knowing the spirit that animates those weapons, or they will destroy you."

I felt an influx of energy from the beautiful women that surrounded me. The colors on their faces blended together in the early morning shadows and moved harmoniously this way and that, like the reflection of a rainbow on a jungle pond. The sadness had left me, and now my heart was full of joy.

"This birthing mask is for you," Jaguar Woman said. She held out a white oval object. It was quite heavy in my hands, and it felt similar to the jaguar mask. I held the face up to the dawn's light. The women were silent. Jaguar Woman put an arm around my shoulder. There were soft tears in my eyes. I clutched the face to me, and then held it out again to look at it. The stone had been carved into a mask shape, but it had no discernible features.

"This mask is a sister to the jaguar mask. It is ancient, and it has been held for centuries in anticipation of the time when the snake appears in the waters broken only by the moon. A time of change has been initiated. There is to be a new face among us that will soon be born. It is yours to choose. There is to be a new face among the Sisterhood of the Shields."

From beyond time,
beyond oak trees and bright clear water flow,
she was given the work of weaving the strands
of her body, her pain, her vision
into creation, and the gift of having created,
to disappear.

Paula Gunn Allen
"Grandmother"

# Chapter 13

# The Obsidian Butterfly

On a bright morning several days later, Agnes, Zoila, and I were seated at breakfast in the hacienda dining room. We had been speaking about the powers of various ancient artifacts. Agnes and Zoila had explained that some artifacts were benevolent, and some were very dangerous.

"These old things, all artifacts, have to be smoked," Agnes said.

"How do you do that?" I asked.

"They must be placed in neutral territory with a circle of tobacco around them. Then you must induce the power to come forward and explain itself. If it has good power, you keep it and use it. If it has bad power, it should be burnt or buried."

Zoila said that her way of smoking magical artifacts was very similar. "I once found a stone killing stick that was over a thousand years old. It had belonged to a black magician and could be used to destroy anyone. When I woke it up it tried to kill me, but luckily José was there. He threw a big piece of red volcanic stone on top of it and trapped its malignant power. We carted it up to the top of a volcano and threw it in. You see, it belonged there. These old sorcerer's tools are nothing to fool around with."

"I'm glad you told me that," I said. "I was about to go explore around some of these old sites and try to find some things of use for my bundles."

"I'm afraid that won't be possible," Zoila said. "That would be

very risky business. You are a spiritually attuned woman, and you
would be exposing yourself to danger unnecessarily. You are at a
precarious point in your apprenticeship. All sorts of dangerous
influences may call out to you, and you don't have the requisite
knowledge to protect yourself. Until you do, you must remain
guarded in your actions."

"Tourists would rarely find such objects," Agnes said. "But you
would probably stumble on many. Pass the tortillas."

I handed her the plate, and she took one.

"You're a magnet right now, Lynn," Zoila chuckled. "One that
draws indiscriminately. You can draw the gruesome as well as the
pleasant."

Agnes spooned up a large bite of melon but paused before eating
it. "That's why it's time for you to leave and go home."

"Agnes, I don't want to leave. I came down here for a vacation. I
want to have some fun."

"Go home, and have your fun," she said after swallowing her bite
of melon. "What was meant to be has been. You were introduced
to the altars, the face of the earth and you have rejoined your
sisters. Now it's time to part." She toyed with another bite of melon
and looked up at me with an inflexible expression. I turned to Zoila,
but her expression was just as immovable.

I felt my cheeks redden. "Well, I guess I really should be back
home working, anyway. I'll go phone the airline for a reservation for
. . ." I looked at them questioningly.

"Tonight," they said in unison.

"Well, at least I have time to finish my tea," I said.

"Go phone now!" Agnes said emphatically.

I got up and walked through the dining room and down the hall
to the phone. The hacienda was silent. No one was around. The
place had a peculiar, echoing emptiness. I phoned the airline and
made a reservation. I had a little more than eight hours to drive
back to Mérida and the airport—plenty of time.

A few minutes later Agnes, Zoila, and I were upstairs packing. I
put my dresses into my carryall bag. "Where are you going, Agnes?
Dare I ask?"

"Take me to Zoila's, please," she said. She was rolling up her few belongings in a blanket, which she tied with a rope. There was a loop on it, which she slung over her shoulder. "Now hurry up."

I raised an eyebrow but made no comment. I would have enjoyed a few days of rest, some time to wander around Uxmal. Carefully, I wrapped and packed my birthing mask and all my other possessions. Zoila and Agnes waited impatiently in the hallway. They kept urging me to hurry, but this only had the effect of disorienting me.

Somehow I felt insecure about leaving so abruptly. I wanted to say goodbye to everyone I had met and recognized as my shield sisters. It had been a couple of years since I had seen them. Perhaps I wanted to be reassured that all of this had indeed actually happened. I felt the covering on the birthing mask for a long moment and zipped up my suitcase. Heaving it up on my shoulder, I quickly joined them.

"I'm glad the Comanches aren't attacking," Agnes said, smiling. "With Lynn along, we would never get out in time to stay alive."

We went down the stairs and outside. I was surprised to see no cars other than mine in the flagstone parking area.

"Where is everyone?" I asked. "Have they left? Where are all the cars that were here?"

"Everyone's shopping," Agnes said.

Zoila's face broke into a smile.

I looked at them curiously. "Shopping?"

"Let them go," Agnes said. "There will be another time."

We all got in the front seat of the car, Agnes in the middle. I drove down the long dirt driveway and onto the narrow jungle road. We said very little. It was a beautiful, sunny day. I watched the colorful birds sailing from tree to tree. I drove slowly, carefully. The jungle was a riot of high coiled vines swimming in green leafy vegetation with long flickering splashes of sunlight and shadow.

We came to the turnoff to Llano and were soon at Zoila's adobe house. We walked up the path together. José came to the door, and we all hugged.

"Leaving so soon, Lynn?" he asked with a smile.

"Orders," I said.

"Yes, it's time," he said.

"First, let's have tea," Zoila said.

Moments later we were all sitting at the wooden table with gourd cups in front of us.

"Where is your Itzpopolotl?" José asked. "The obsidian butterfly. I want to see her. You should wear her around your neck on your way home for protection."

I was startled by the question. "Oh my, I don't know. Agnes and Zoila have been rushing me around so much, I must have put it in my pipe bag."

"Well, go out to the car and get it," Agnes said.

I ran outside. I didn't know exactly where it was. I rummaged through everything, becoming frantic. I was sure I had put it in my pipe bag, but it wasn't there. I took everything out of my bags, draped my clothes over the front seat, and put my shoes and other items on the hood. Beside myself, I ran back into the house.

"Did you find her?" José asked.

Everyone was looking at me expectantly.

"Well?" Agnes said.

I shook my head. "No, I must have taken it off to bathe and left it on the sink. I'll drive back right now. I'll see you in a few minutes."

I gave Agnes's arm a squeeze, and I was out the door when I heard José call after me, "Wait a minute. You'd better let us go with you."

"It's no trouble. I can do it."

I ran to the car and was soon roaring through the jungle toward the hacienda. It felt totally different driving by myself. It seemed like an inordinate amount of time had passed, and I still hadn't reached the hacienda. Then I realized I had been driving for half an hour. I turned the car around as soon as I could and sped back in the direction I had come from. This time I checked the road carefully. The jungle seemed to look different, darker somehow. I drove up and down the road where I was sure the hacienda should be located. Back and forth I drove, turning the car around again and again and backtracking. Either I was having a nervous breakdown,

which wouldn't have surprised me after all that had happened, or I
was driving blindly right by the hacienda. Finally I stopped the car.
I was so exasperated that I pounded on the steering wheel. After
checking my watch, I found that I had been driving around in
circles for two hours!

"Now calm down, Lynn," I said to myself. "You've made some
simple mistake, that's all. Hurry back to Zoila's, so you won't miss
your plane. Maybe they can all go back to the hacienda with you."

I was greatly happy to see Llano, though the village seemed to
have changed considerably—in what way, I wasn't exactly sure. As I
approached Zoila's house, a deep, grinding fear took hold of my
belly. The house was in ruins! I pulled the car to a stop and gaped
at the structure. The roof had collapsed, the beams lying askew on a
grassy mound of adobe. It looked like the place hadn't been lived in
for years. Saplings were growing inside. A little white goat peeked its
head from around the corner of what had been the kitchen—the
kitchen where I had left Agnes, Zoila, and José not three hours
before!

I was terrified. I began to inhale great breaths of air, gasping. I
sobbed uncontrollably. I had finally done it—I had lost my mind. I
managed to see my watch through my tear-brimmed eyes. It had
stopped. A weariness seemed to clutch me. I saw an old woman
coming up the road. She was wrapped in a shawl. I ran up and
asked her if she knew Zoila and José Gutierez. I pointed frantically
at the ruined house.

She didn't speak English.

Another old woman, dressed similarly, came rushing over to us.

"Can I help you, señora?" she asked.

I asked her if she knew Zoila and José Guiterez.

"Oh yes," she answered. "I remember they used to live in that
house. That was a long time ago."

"How long ago was it?"

"About forty years, I think."

I was shaking all over, and the old woman grabbed hold of my
arm to steady me.

"Is there something I can do for you, señora?" she asked.

"No. I mean yes. Who owns this house now?"

"We do. Zoila and José sold it to us years ago. We use it now for our goats."

"For goats," I repeated more to myself than to the two women. They were staring at me like I was a madwoman. "No!" I shouted. "What's happening to me?"

They tried to hold me back, but I ran toward the fallen house. I was stopped by a barbed wire fence. I tried to crawl through it, putting a long scratch down my leg. I tore my skirt, and the cut began to bleed.

"Now see what you've done, señora. What is wrong?" The old woman knelt down beside me. Her eyes were very kind. The other old woman dabbed at my leg with a rag.

"I knew these people," I tried to explain.

"What people?"

"Gutierez," I managed to say.

"I hardly think this is possible. They left here forty years ago." She spoke gently.

"Where did they go?"

"I don't know. Some people say they went way up north to Canada."

"Canada! I love them," I said. "It just can't be."

"You would have been a child, señora."

"Do you know of a big hacienda down the road?" I pointed and then wiped the tears from my cheeks.

"Hacienda?"

"Yes, a big one about fifteen minutes from here on the right."

"Child," the woman said, "I've heard tales of such a hacienda, but the jungle took it before you were born. No one from this village will go near there. They say there are ghosts and night stalkers, and even the devil himself resides there. But there is nothing there today, only jungle and henequen fields for fifty miles."

It was becoming evident to me, astonishing as it was, that I had somehow breached a gap in time. Many extraordinary things had happened to me since I had become the apprentice of Agnes Whistling Elk, but this was the strangest of all. I tried to be calm in

spite of everything. I tried to quiet my thumping heart and stop the
avalanche of questions hurtling through my mind.

I asked mechanically, "Which way is Mérida? Does it still exist?"

"Of course it exists. I was there, well, fourteen or so months ago."

"Thank you for your kindness," I said. "You've helped me a great
deal. Do you mind if I stay here for a while, maybe sit over in the
ruin for just a bit before I leave?"

She smiled. "Of course not. If you need anything, we live in the
house over there." She pointed to a thatched-roof adobe.

"I'll be fine," I said.

The women left me, and I stepped through the barbed wire
fence. I strolled around the relic of a house. Not much remained.
Finally I sat down on a fallen, rotted viga. I was stunned, numbed. I
remained until late in the night. The sky was clouded, and there was
only one single star to keep me company. (It was the star I had
chosen as my own, the star Zoila had shown me.) I couldn't see very
far in any direction. I heard a rustling sound and saw two enormous
female figures approaching me. They were bathed in a blue flamelike
light. Nothing surprised me anymore.

"We have come with a message from your teacher and friends,"
the tall blue-lighted figure on my left said.

"Tell me," I said.

"José said to tell you, 'sorry for the inconvenience.' He tried to
warn you."

"Are they all right? Agnes? Zoila? José?"

"They said to tell you that you can count on meeting them
again."

The blue figures of the women started to recede.

"Wait. How did all this happen?"

I stood up, but the figures were gone, leaving me in the inky
darkness.

I stumbled over the barbed wire fence to my car and started it.

we can find all the fallen stars
and place them
           among the leaves
                        where the branches

lay hidden, almost
tangled in the dark

           Sheila Ross
           "The Tree in the Dark"

# Chapter 14
# The Eternal Return

The cold, howling wind outside protested and lashed against the cabin. The windows were completely frosted over. The logs in the stove had burnt to embers, and a deep chill had invaded us all. July threw some wood inside the stove and poked it with an iron rod until flames were leaping. We all squeezed closer to the fire, inclining our chairs to the best advantage.

Telling my experiences had made me cry. I blew my reddened nose. We all seemed mesmerized by the blaze that crackled and spit. It threw an embroidery of dancing orange light over the entire room. I could sense Ruby's impatience. For many long minutes we sat in silence, each with our private thoughts.

"I'm sorry," July piped up. "I can't understand what happened to Zoila and José."

"I'm just telling you what happened to me. I don't know what happened to them. All I know is that they had moved nearly forty years ago."

"What about the hacienda?" July asked. "Where did it go?"

"We tried to warn her," Agnes said. "Unwittingly, Lynn fell out of harmony with our doubling. Had she not lost the Itzpopolotl and had to leave, she would have been in harmony with us, and everything would have been fine."

"What is 'doubling'?" July asked timidly.

"All I know is that it happens," I answered.

July and I looked at Agnes.

"Good question," she said. "To answer that we must explore time. Time is born of what you call the ego and what we call the self lodge. The ego is the illusion of form. To remain in form one must have a concept of time because of the similarity of the two. Time is a construct of the mind, because the mind is ego. It desperately holds onto time and clutches it like a tyrant, because it wants to survive. Once you leap the boundaries of time and step into timelessness, you step into the sacred dream wheel, where the ego is no longer needed. The ego is an entity that struggles for survival and fears the loss of form, because it knows it will die."

"I see you're in good form tonight, Agnes," Ruby said sarcastically.

"Go on, Agnes," I urged.

"Lynn, you often speak of 'karma.' If a great teacher chooses to stay on this earth to teach, she may take on karma in order to stay in form. Once you release the mind from karma, you have the ability to step out of time into formlessness. That is the law of doubling, the process of remirroring from one round to another. Leaping over karma, you are able to be in more places than one. The world hasn't changed. Your self lodge has. Why do you suppose you see great women or men of knowledge who have addictions to alcohol or food?"

"I don't know. I can't imagine."

"Because addictions are karma, and they keep you nailed down on this earthly plane. They keep you in form."

"Words!" Ruby said obnoxiously. "Beans, if you ask me."

Agnes reached for the dim kerosene lantern and took it from its place on the floor. She pumped it up and held it glowing brightly over her head. "Words are beans," Agnes said. "But there is an illumination of higher knowledge. The true answer, that which illuminates us, is within. It illuminates in a new way even that which is clearly seen."

"Get that lamp away from me, Agnes," Ruby said irritably. "It hurts my eyes."

"Well, I believe I stepped out of time in some way," I said.

"Do you expect an intelligent woman like me to believe this cock-and-bull story you told us?" Ruby cut in. "I think both of you are pulling my leg. From Lynn, I expect it. But from you, Agnes. It's just like you to take advantage of an old blind woman and try to make a fool out of her."

"Don't get angry, Ruby," I implored. "I *am* telling you the truth. That's the way it happened."

"I'm mad, and I'm going to stay mad!" Ruby shouted. "You were walking around with your eyes closed, that's all."

"No, I wasn't!"

"Admit it, Lynn. You were lost. White people don't have a sense of direction," Ruby said with her customary harshness. "We Indians always get up on a hill or a tree or a roof or something, so we'll know where we're at."

The wind outside murmured and blew greedily. I wasn't going to argue with Ruby. I knew what had happened to me. July followed the conversation wide-eyed with a bewildered expression on her face. Agnes remained patient. I pushed my chair back and began to rummage through my things. I found my birthing mask and brought it over to Ruby.

"You know I'm blind. What have you got there?" she demanded. She snatched it out of my hands and examined it. "Feels like an old rock."

"Ruby, that's the birthing mask I was telling you about."

She turned her face to mine, and I looked into her terrifying, luminous eyes. "Nonsense! You show me a piece of rock and try to make me swallow it." She seemed repulsed and shoved the mask back into my hands. "Get away from me!" She got up, pulled her shawl tightly around her shoulders, and started pacing up and down. She had a scowl on her face, and it was so cold that tendrils of steam came from her nose.

A freezing blast of wind struck the cabin. The walls creaked. I was tormentingly aware of the chill and getting tired. Stoically I rose to get ready for bed.

"I suppose you're going to sleep now, Lynn," Ruby said in a grumbling voice.

I turned to her, sensing that she was up to something.

"Come here," she said. "I want to return something to you."

I walked over to her. She reached in her pocket and rummaged around, taking a great deal of time. The pocket wasn't that large. Finally she held out her hand to me and dropped a leather pouch into my palm.

"For me?"

"Open it," Ruby said.

I pulled the ties apart and shook it. A butterfly cocoon fell out. My eyes widened. I opened it and held the Itzpopolotl to the lamplight. Bending down, I touched the obsidian wings. "I just—I can't believe it, Ruby!" I stammered.

"Isn't that what you were looking for?" She winked at me and smiled for the first time that day. "Go to sleep, Lynn."

That night I was restless. I was cold and got up time and time again to put more wood on the fire. It seemed to barely heat the cabin. My thoughts were of Ruby and the gift she had given me. I never knew what to expect from her. I even wondered if she were the Jaguar Woman—same height, same proud carriage, same basic features. But then that would have been impossible.

At dawn, wearing snowshoes and dressed as warmly as we could manage, we trekked to a small lake about two miles away. We spent hours chopping a hole in the ice. We fed our baited fishing lines into the hole, and the fish bit like mad. Soon we had as much as the four of us could carry. We trudged back to the cabin over the snowswept icy tundra.

About halfway there we stopped to rest and eat some of our raw catch. It was a well-earned meal, and everyone ate their fill.

"This is a good day," Agnes said, sweeping her black eyes over the frigid landscape. "The chill will break soon."

"How do you know that, Agnes?" I asked.

"I can feel it inside my body. The blizzards are over. It's something you know when you live up here for many winters."

Ruby threw a fish scrap onto the pile of bones. She wiped her mouth with the back of her mitten. July was sitting with her legs straight out in front of her, scooping snow into a gallon-sized tin can with a knife. She got a can of sterno from her bag and lit it with a lighter. The she held the sterno can with her mittened hand to melt the snow for tea. Eventually she handed each of us the larger can, filled now with pine needle tea. I sipped the tea, and it tasted wonderful.

"Are you wearing your Itzpopolotl, Lynn?" Ruby asked.

"I sure am," I said, putting my hand on my parka. "I don't think I'll lose it this time."

July and Ruby beamed at me.

We finished the tea and started back toward the cabin. It was steep going, and we left large tracks. The wind shifted and carried off the surface snow in wildly dancing and leaping patterns. Agnes stopped at the bottom of a slick hillside.

"Ruby, you and July go on," she said. "I want Lynn to come with me."

We were about a half mile from the cabin. We huddled together briefly, laughing and clowning, and then July and Ruby went on. I watched them depart, their silhouettes standing out against the shiny snow.

"Come on," Agnes said.

"Where are we going?" I asked.

"To the tree," she said.

"To the butterfly tree?"

"Yes, I want to pay my respects."

I moved up beside her. Agnes walked skillfully in snowshoes, and I, clumsily. The wind whipped the snow into wraiths again. The horizon was now an angry, spread-out, red color. We came to the end of a clearing and then went down onto a white plateau. The butterfly tree was in sight. Agnes insisted we approach from the east. We both gave the trunk a big hug. The ice-covered skin of the tree was yellowish and disfigured. The wind was whistling musically. The way Agnes was carrying on, it was as though she were greeting a long lost friend.

I asked her about it.

She sat on the ground and patted the snow for me to sit down next to her. "She *is* a long lost friend, Lynn," she said.

"How's that?"

"The ancients have wisely spoken of the sacred tree. Almost all peoples know of some kind of world tree."

"Like the tree of good and evil in the Bible?"

"Yes, the tree is a way into life. There are many trees, Lynn, and many myths and legends concerning them. Right now I would like to tell you another of these myths. Always look for the truth beyond the words. The Sisterhood of the Shields tells us of the first tree, also called Sky Tree of Man, or simply, the butterfly tree. This is the tree of all the ancestors; it is where first man and first woman came from. Tree Mother suckled them.

"The sisters say that upon the branches of this tree are billions and billions of leaves. Written upon these leaves is the destiny of each new person. So when a person is born, a leaf falls from the butterfly tree. The spirit light descends from one of these leaves and surrounds the egg at conception.

"It is a person's destiny to realize that we are one with the sacred tree. We are not just a leaf. We are light. And we are the light of Butterfly Tree. Everything is of Butterfly Tree, and all will return to it. All suffering is a result of a loss of knowledge of our origins. When we realize that we are the great tree, our state is happiness. All your illusions come about because of loss of remembering the central tree."

"But Agnes, is this one tree or many trees?"

"It is no tree at all. It is a way of explaining truth."

"What about my experiences in the Butterfly Tree?"

"I spoke of the truth behind my words. You have died the death of a shamaness. When we enter the void, it's like no place we have ever been before. That's a problem. Our language is inadequate to express the higher truths that we come back with. Some people see angels; some see warriors. Some call these beings gods and goddesses. Some call them spirits.

"The human mind is unable to grasp these experiences. That doesn't mean it is delusion. As a matter of fact, we are escaping our delusions. There are other ways of seeing. All of life is a trail that leads to the Great Tree or the Great Spirit. Everyone is on this path. Some are, for the moment, lost. Some are resting. Some realize the truth but can go no further.

"Every once in a while a great teacher comes. Great teachers are the realized ones. They are the noble chiefs and leaders who have conquered all illusion, all maya. They have climbed the Tree and have achieved freedom. They have solved the riddle of paradox and duality. They can speak only truth. But even they have difficulty in trying to explain things in a way others can understand. Some of them get mad and use supernatural powers all over the place, thinking that this may help. Others martyr themselves to show their great love and tolerance. Some of them don't do anything at all and let everything go on as it is. They may be hidden in a cave or sacred mountain, or they may be your next-door neighbor."

"And what does a butterfly represent, Agnes?"

Agnes searched my face with her kind eyes. "I remember when I was young, a little girl, some old people told me a story that I believe to this day. They said that the Great Spirit had made the butterfly to show us how to live."

"And how is that, Agnes?"

"The life of the caterpillar transforms into another life—the beautiful butterfly. It teaches us that all of life is transitory. The butterfly is enlightened! Another gift from the Great Spirit. You see, they are the ancestor spirits, and they have returned to the Butterfly Tree. The Great Spirit permits these beings before they leave this world to return one last time to the places of the ceremonies, the sacred places, where as humans they had found great joy. Where the butterflies cluster on a tree, this was one of the ancient sites where rituals and ceremonies were performed, places of celebration."

"Have the butterflies come again to celebrate life?" I asked.

"Whenever you see a butterfly, you should feel a gladness in your heart. Yes, the butterfly migrations are ancient spirits returning to the sites of once great cultures that have now vanished from the earth.

"The Great Spirit gave the world a butterfly tree so that the people could learn from it and find joy in its beauty. The tree was filled with colors, and those colors formed rainbows that arched from

one camp to another and from one universe to another. The people
were united, because they saw the same colors. From this rainbow
hung the stars, the moon, the sun, the seven sisters, and the
movement of all the heavenly bodies."

"And you believe this?"

"Very much."

"I believe it too," I said.

We sat close together under the tree, under the naked dark
branches. I felt oddly happy, content, just sitting next to my
teacher. I realized I was shivering from the violent cold. Agnes stood
and drew me up with her. We turned toward her cabin.

"I'll remember to be happy the next time I see a butterfly," I
said.

Agnes released my arm. Her eyes swept over the vast snowy
landscape, the northern lights drawing a flowing curtain of yellow,
red, and purple across the sky. She looked back at me.

"They'll be here soon, Lynn. And life will begin again."